IMAGES
of America

DELAWARE HORSE RACING

It was once said that Austin "Ned" Galentine was a brilliant horseman, one of those guys who "spoke horse" and could really get inside the animals' heads. Pictured above, Galentine and his racehorse Mr. Regal are in the lead in the home stretch at Brandywine Raceway on August 2, 1971. (Courtesy Harrington Historical Society.)

On the Cover: In the late afternoon with the sun setting in the west, Mr. Regal is leading the first race. He came down the stretch to the finish line, winning in 2:05 for owner Flowing Acres and starting the evening race card at Brandywine Raceway with trainer and driver Austin "Ned" Galentine in the bike on August 2, 1971. (Courtesy of Harrington Historical Society.)

IMAGES
of America

DELAWARE HORSE RACING

Lacey Lafferty

ARCADIA
PUBLISHING

ISBN 978-0-7385-9763-8

Published by Arcadia Publishing
Charleston, South Carolina

Printed in the United States of America

Library of Congress Control Number: 2012939072

For all general information, please contact Arcadia Publishing:
Telephone 843-853-2070
Fax 843-853-0044
E-mail sales@arcadiapublishing.com
For customer service and orders:
Toll-Free 1-888-313-2665

Visit us on the Internet at www.arcadiapublishing.com

I dedicate this book to the horses, for without them there would be no sport. They deserve our respect, admiration, and continued commitment to enhance their quality of life through their career and retirement.

Contents

ACKNOWLEDGMENTS

The purpose of this book is to preserve and document Delaware's long history of accomplishments in horse racing. Like any endeavor, this book could not have been completed without assistance from the following people who provided vital historical information and photographs: Michael Wirtschafter, Miller family historian; Matt Sparacino, assistant general manager of Harrington Raceway; Vicky Brenneman; Brenda Lewis Bramble; Wayne Wilkins; Rosalie Walls, Georgetown Historical Society/Nutter Marvel Museum; Richard Calhoun; William Sink; Ellen Rendel, Delaware Historical Society; Jean Miller, Harrington Historical Society; Joe Ann Adams, Melvin Joseph family historian; Hazell Smith; Heather Moffett; Rebecca Batson Kidner, granddaughter of Luther Lyons; Eddie Lambden; Scott Peck; Lou Johnson; Roman Miller; and all the people of Delaware horse racing who have assisted with this endeavor. I thank my daughter Lacey Lynn, the love of my life, who—at seven years old and with her love for horses—allowed me to sacrifice our together time and understood my ambition to complete the book.

Introduction

This book tells a story of the First State of Delaware's involvement in horse racing. Delaware not only has a rich history of industrial legacies, but it also has a vast history of small, dirt racetracks that sprang up in all three counties, materializing into the three major horse racetracks of today.

Delaware is not a very big state in comparison to the rest of America, but what it lacks in size, it makes up for with down-home ingenuity. Delaware may not be Kentucky, but it is definitely horse country. In the northern part of the state with its rolling hills, hot-blooded Thoroughbreds race on turf and dirt; through the flatlands of Kent and Sussex County, Standardbreds are used for racing, showing, pleasure, and everyday transportation. Horses have been racing in matinees and fairs across America for the last 150 years. Matinee and fair racing is still going strong in surrounding states, such as Pennsylvania, New York, Ohio, and Maine.

In the early 1900s, all breeds of horses had a purpose in Delaware, but none had one like the Standardbred and Thoroughbred racehorses. Fair tracks sprang up in rural farm fields throughout Delaware, including Elsmere (northern part of the state), Kent and Sussex County Fairgrounds–Harrington Raceway (middle part of the state), and Myers Raceway in Bridgeville (southwestern part of Sussex County), which laid the foundation of horse racing as it is known today.

Kent and Sussex County Fairgrounds was formed in 1919 by a group of individuals that was meeting around an old woodstove in a railroad station in Harrington. Ideas began to emerge through consecutive meetings, until a purchase of 30 acres was made from Willie and Nellie Smith at the cost of $6,000 on February 17, 1920. The first fair ran for four nights and four days in July 1920 with a carnival in the midway. Harness racing was the main attraction, which brought thousands of people from all over the state to watch Delaware's finest trainers and drivers maneuver the new, half-mile track.

As years passed and new attractions became a focal point in drawing more people to the fair, the board purchased more land to expand its exhibits. Racehorse purses increased to draw better and more competitive horses. In the early 1940s, when the war began, fair operations and horse racing were ceased by a request from the Office of Transportation to postpone fair activities as a war conservation measure regarding patron safety. The fair resumed a couple of years later, and in 1946, the Kent and Sussex Racing Association was organized to hold pari-mutuel racing, and paddock and stables were built. In 1967, the Kent and Sussex County Raceway changed its name to the Harrington Raceway.

There were several independently owned dirt tracks in farm fields around the state as well. People had a need for entertainment, and horse racing filled that need through the hard times of the Depression and both of the world wars. Delaware Park Raceway's one-mile dirt track opened on June 26, 1937, with a 30-day meet and seating for 7,500 people in the grandstand. Outstanding features of Delaware Park Raceway were its exquisite architecture as well as the saddling and picnic grove areas.

Many tracks were created from farmers' fields in the 1920s, 1930s, and 1940s in lower Delaware. Some of the local dirt tracks had a dual purpose: automobile racing and matinee-fair horse racing. These tracks included Beaverdam Training Center in Roxana, Myers Raceway in Bridgeville, Delmarva Raceway in Georgetown, and L.B. Brittingham Raceway in Laurel. Back in the day, area horsemen, such as Gardner Bryan, Henry Chipman, and L.B. Brittingham, acquired horses for trainer Allen Myer along with other owners and trainers, including Charles Marsh, Paul Short, Richard Calhoun, and Mel Wilkins, and campaigned their racehorses across Sussex County. Charles H. Wilkins and his son Elwood "Boots" Wilkins created one such half-mile oval horse track called Delmarva Raceway, later called Georgetown Raceway, located on US Route 9 east of Georgetown. Thousands of people would come from all over to cheer on their favorite drivers and racehorses. Drivers included Jack Parker, Edward Long, Richard Lewis, J.D. Dennis, Donald Shockley, James Stewart, Ervin Miller, Charles Laws, James Manaway, and Jim Adkins. Trainers fielded the races with top-notch Standardbred racehorse talent from nearby Doulby Breeding Farm, operated by Goal, Jack, and Harley Doulby, throughout the 1950s and 1960s. Racehorse purses were $500 in 1971, a contrast to the present-day purses at Dover Downs Raceway and Harrington Raceway. Today, Georgetown Raceway still stands in the shadow of its former glory.

On September 10, 1953, Nathan and Howard Miller opened Brandywine Raceway to an unexpected crowd of 16,000 people eager to see the new facility just outside of Wilmington in the Brandywine Valley of New Castle County. Brandywine Raceway soon became the hot spot of nightly horse racing entertainment and was where celebrities and politicians visited frequently. Not to be outdone, Brandywine Raceway started experiencing growing pains in the 1960s, and it expanded its raceway from a half-mile to five-eighths of a mile and renovated the grandstand from 16,000 seats to over 25,000. The Battle of the Brandywine was its premier racing event, which would draw the best horses and drivers on the East Coast.

In the mid-1960s, three men who were familiar with racing—John W. Rollins, Melvin Joseph, and Dave P. Buckson—came together as a group and formed Dover Downs. The group purchased a farm owned by Thomas Murray on the east side of Dover. Joseph, who owned a construction company, engineered the design and built the NASCAR track and horse racetrack (located within the NASCAR track), which had its debut in 1969. Today, Dover Downs showcases some of the fastest racehorses on the East Coast and features races like the Progress Pace, Matron Series, the Classic Series, and the Delaware Standardbred Breeders' Fund Stakes (DSBF).

Found in Delaware horse racing are the families who have been involved in the sport for generations. People get involved in the sport through their parents, grandparents, and great-grandparents. Family involvement runs deep in Delaware racing. One such family is the Gardner Bryan family from Laurel, Delaware. Gardner Bryan owned several Standardbred racehorses trained by Allen Myer that raced at area tracks throughout Sussex County. Eventually, Gardner handed the reins down to his granddaughter Brenda Lewis Bramble to carry on the family tradition. Brenda picked up where Gardner left off, submerging herself in not only racing horses, but also representing the horsemen as well. Brenda is currently the vice president of the Delaware Standardbreds Owners Association (DSOA), where she has held an active presence for 17 years. Brenda's two sons, Doug and Darrell Lewis, are carrying on the family tradition with separate successful racing stables of their own.

Even though some of the old racetracks have disappeared, the long, rich history of the three remaining horse racetracks—Delaware Park Raceway, Dover Downs Raceway, and Harrington Raceway—are still very much on solid ground since the establishment of the casinos. The financial support of the casinos for each racetrack has enabled the horsemen's purses to increase, where owners, trainers, and drivers can benefit from a profitable income. Horse racing contributes to other related employment opportunities, including feed stores, mechanical parts and supplies, farm equipment sales, farrier services, equine veterinarians, barn and paddock employment, truck and horse trailer sales, employment at the racetracks, and employment for the Delaware Racing Commission racetrack personnel, which operates under the Department of Agriculture for the State of Delaware. Employment opportunities exist due to Delaware horse racing, and the industry should be preserved for future generations to seek a career that is as a wholesome as the farmers who started the sport over a century ago. Through the years, Delaware race tracks have changed their names eliminating raceway from their names such as Dover Downs and Delaware Park.

Delaware horse racing will continue to be passed on to the next generation as long as family values remain strong enough to endure the ups and downs that exist in the horse racing industry. Most horsemen and horsewomen will tell you that it is their love for the horses that gives them the determination to continue their career. It is my desire to inspire you with memories or knowledge of Delaware's racehorse history within the photographs and events described in this book.

One

Kicking Up the Dirt

Before the 1900s and the automobile revolution, horses were the mode of transportation for thousands of years. The Romans conducted chariot races in the Coliseum before thousands of people for their pleasure and entertainment. They treated their equine athletes lavishly, sparing no expense for the horse's care and well-being.

Between the 1600s and the 1900s, horses were the primary means of transportation and instrumental in developing the United States as it is today. In Delaware, like the rest of the nation, horses were used to haul goods from destination to destination (whether several miles or several hundred miles), pull farm equipment in the fields, and travel to social functions and church-related activities. Today, through western Kent County, the Amish still use horses for their everyday needs.

Whether riding horseback or driving a horse-and-buggy along the rural dirt roads of Delaware, before the 1900s, one can only imagine the conversations between friends and strangers as they met and passed one another along the trails. Perhaps they struck up dialogue that consisted of, "I bet my horse can beat your horse," or, "My horse is faster than your horse," which resulted in horse racing as it is known today.

As the early 20th century progressed, horse racing was propelled toward other areas of the state. Farmer's fields were used for horse racing, and matinees and fairs were scheduled for the community's entertainment. The people within these close-knit communities depended on their horse-and-buggy for travel while also utilizing the same horses for racing on the weekends.

As time passed into the late 1900s, popularity of horse racing increased. People formed organizations and held matinees and fairs to accommodate the ever-increasing demand for the sport. One such fair, the Kent and Sussex County Fair, was created in 1919 from a purchase of 30 acres for $6,000 and located in Harrington, Delaware. Harness racing was conducted on what was considered by racing officials to be one of the best half-mile tracks and grounds to be found anywhere in the East. The fair organizers knew they had a product. It would provide wholesome, family entertainment that would draw thousands of people from hundreds of miles. Due to the last 100 years of perfecting the tradition, today's horse racing has propelled into super stardom from the mere words from long ago, "I bet my horse is faster than your horse."

The center of Georgetown is unusual among other municipalities in Delaware; in the middle of town is a park surrounded by a road. Known as "The Circle," it is the location of the town hall and state and county buildings, the historic Sussex County Courthouse, and stores like Marshall and Chipman's Drug Store (formerly Layton and Layton) pictured here in 1900–1910 with residents gathered in front. The current courthouse was built in 1837 on South Bedford Street, replacing the original structure. Georgetown Historical Society currently manages and further restored the structure in 1976. Within the center of Georgetown's circle today is a petite park with a charming fountain, outlined with banks, stores, and lawyers' offices. (Courtesy of Georgetown Historical Society/Nutter Marvel Museum.)

In the early 1900s, a faded portrait of the Brick Hotel located on the historical circle of Georgetown depicts what was a focal point of busy activity among county residents and people traveling through the state. The Brick Hotel was recently restored and modernized into a restaurant. Two days after Election Day, every two years, Georgetown presents a unique event recognized as Returns Day. Festivities include a parade, ox roast, and several businesses peddling their merchandises. Since Colonial days, the public would ride on horseback and assemble in the circle of Georgetown two days after the election to hear the results. The winners of the election year's races ride in carriages in a parade around the Circle, and the losers along with the political party chairs ceremonially "bury the hatchet" in a bucket of sand. Returns Day afternoon is a holiday in Sussex County for state and county workers and is celebrated with festivities and merriment toward future political campaigns. (Courtesy of Georgetown Historical Society/Nutter Marvel Museum.)

The grandeur of the white marble building of the Farmers Bank is pictured on the right. The uniquely crafted Eagle Hotel across the street and the Sussex County Courthouse surround the Circle. People throughout the county traveled by horse-and-buggy in the early 1900s. (Courtesy of Georgetown Historical Society/Nutter Marvel Museum.)

People are pictured in the early 1900s meeting one another at the Eagle Hotel, which was located on the southeast corner of the Circle. They are most likely socializing about everyday activities, job opportunities, and area recreation, which included horse racing just out of town limits. The Eagle Hotel was torn down in 1932 to make way for the post office, now the Sussex County Administration Building. (Courtesy of Georgetown Historical Society/Nutter Marvel Museum.)

Looking south on North Bedford Street towards the Circle in 1895, several horse-and-buggy tracks indicate excessive use of the road into Georgetown. In the distance on the right is a church, where the Georgetown Presbyterian Church campus is located today. (Courtesy of Georgetown Historical Society/Nutter Marvel Museum.)

Between 1910 and 1920, L.W. Pollitt's Country Store on the outskirts of Georgetown transitioned to selling gasoline to area residents who were slowly switching from horse-and-buggies to automobiles. The country store also served dual purposes, with the store in the front of the building and living quarters in the rear. (Courtesy of Georgetown Historical Society/Nutter Marvel Museum.)

In the heat of the day during the early 1900s, an unidentified driver of an ice wagon and its occupants deliver ice from the Harrington Ice Company to the area of Short Street in Harrington. Houses in this photograph are still there today. (Courtesy of Harrington Historical Society.)

When a county event took place in the early 1900s, such as the hanging of Jim Gordy on South Bedford Street just off the Circle in Georgetown, pictured above, people gathered and used the event to socialize with neighbors. (Courtesy of Georgetown Historical Society/Nutter Marvel Museum.)

Norman Wilkins (driving seat), Marshall Wilkins (sitting in the front), Asher Wilkins (sitting in the back), and Boots Wilkins (standing in the back of carriage) are pictured in the 1920s arriving at Rueben Savage's County Fair farm and racetrack. Rueben's was located on the northeast corner of US Route 9 and Sandhill Road, east of Georgetown. (Courtesy of Georgetown Historical Society/Nutter Marvel Museum.)

A group of men in the 1920s on a sunny afternoon at an unidentified racetrack are congratulating the winner in front of hundreds of spectators. (Courtesy of Georgetown Historical Society/Nutter Marvel Museum.)

After a long week, hardworking people in the 1920s are dressed in their best clothes for a weekend afternoon at the horse races. Lynn and Amelia Ritter (right) are pictured with an unidentified couple in the Lewes area. (Author's collection.)

Between 1900 and 1920, area racetracks had various kinds of classifications for entries, including four-wheel and two-wheel racing carts. The name of the Standardbred horse pictured is Willy, and he won his four-wheel race in 2:05. (Courtesy of Georgetown Historical Society/Nutter Marvel Museum.)

Georgetown horseman and driver Rueben Savage held county fairs at his farm's racetrack, located on the northeast corner of US Route 9 and Sandhill Road east of Georgetown, in the 1930s. In the photograph, Reuben is driving his racehorse in a fair race on his farm's racetrack. (Courtesy of Harrington Historical Society.)

Horseman and driver Rueben Savage is pictured at his residence in Georgetown. In the 1930s, he held matinees and fairs at his farm to help area farmers and horsemen utilize their horses from weekly work into weekend entertainment. (Courtesy of Harrington Historical Society.)

On an early spring day in the 1920s, Ernest L. Derrickson (grandfather of Donald Derrickson) is pictured at an unidentified racetrack holding on to his horse after a warm-up session in Kent County. Notice the early model vehicle between the two gentlemen. (Courtesy of Harrington Historical Society.)

In a fair race at an unidentified racetrack in Kent County in 1920, Ernest L. Derrickson drove his horse Brownie Girl to a win in 2:15.5. Racetracks were carved out of farmers' cornfields; a field of corn can be seen in the background of this photograph. (Courtesy of Harrington Historical Society.)

In the late 1940s, Delaware had a harness horse superstar with Fred Greenly Sr.'s horse Direct Express. The Billy Direct stallion campaigned regularly on the Grand Circuit, racing at Roosevelt Raceway and setting a new track record of 2:01 on August 15, 1947, as a three year old. Unfortunately, Direct Express would meet an untimely death in California later in the year, ending an outstanding career. He was buried in the infield of Roosevelt Raceway. (Courtesy of Harrington Historical Society.)

Owners Reese B. Harrington and Alta Coffin Harrington look over their racehorse My Scott, sired by Blackhawk in the 1940s. In 1945, during a new adventure and the beginning of a milestone, Kent and Sussex Raceway formed a committee and, headed by Sen. Fred Bailey, negotiated for pari-mutuel racing. (Courtesy of Harrington Historical Society.)

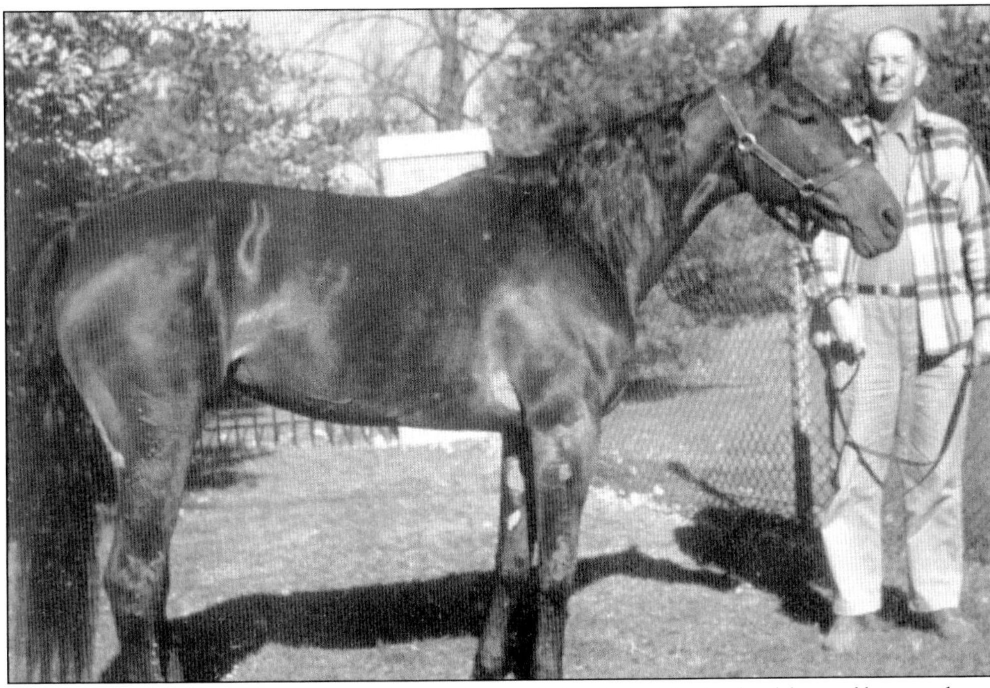

On a leisurely stroll through the yard in 1949, Carl Goslin holds the lead line of his racehorse Majestic Miss. The racehorse's regular driver was Luther Lyons of Greenwood, Delaware. (Courtesy of Harrington Historical Society.)

Edwin "Eddie" Myer, the oldest of the Myer's nine boys, all of whom raced on the peninsula, had a family farm and racing stable in Bridgeville. The Myer family became a local legend, holding matinees and fairs at their racetrack in the afternoons. The Myer boys dominated racing on the Eastern Shore with spectacular driving moves that allowed the racehorse to gain an advantage. (Courtesy of Harrington Historical Society.)

J. Howard Lyons of Greenwood, Delaware, purchased Adios Harry in 1952 for $4,200 at a yearling sale in Mechanicsburg, Pennsylvania, not knowing he would end up with a world champion in five years. Delaware resident Adios Harry's greatness had emerged into his three-year-old racing career in 1954, with nine wins, four seconds, and a world record in the Little Brown Jug with 19 starts. (Courtesy of Rebecca Batson Kidner.)

The Lyons family members pictured are J. Howard Lyons (right), Luther Lyons (middle), and John Lyons (kneeling). In 1955, J. Howard recognized how important Adios Harry was to the family business and made a driver change, handing the reins over to his son Luther Lyons. On July 16, 1955, Luther would drive Adios Harry to the world record at New York's Vernon Downs Raceway in 1:55. (Courtesy of Rebecca Batson Kidner.)

Breaking several world records by July 16, 1955, Adios Harry was named Aged Pacer of the Year, and his 1:55 record race mile was not broken until more than a decade later by Albatross in 1971. Adios Harry held 12 world records, 59 wins, and won over $345,000 in his outstanding career, which spanned six years. (Courtesy of Rebecca Batson Kidner.)

Luther Lyons once stated, "Harry was a just a muscleman, he liked to go out and race and win." When Adios Harry's racing career ended in 1958, he was returned to J. Howard's horse farm, Sugar Hill, in Greenwood, Delaware, to stand stud until he was in his late 20s. J. Howard is pictured in 1956, holding Adios Harry at the Sugar Hill Farm. (Courtesy of Rebecca Batson Kidner.)

Adios Harry won several races, setting several world records throughout his illustrious career. His racing accomplishments would continue for the Lyons family, as Harry was honored with a special award by the Delaware Standardbred Owners Association after being a recent inductee into the Harness Racing Hall of Fame in 2001 as an immortal. Dolores Batson accepted the honor on behalf her late grandfather J. Howard and father, Luther Lyons. (Courtesy of Rebecca Batson Kidner.)

World champion Adios Harry was the first animal to be on the cover of *Sports Illustrated*, on July 23, 1956. While in retirement, Adios Harry would enjoy an occasional chew of tobacco from Luther Lyons and stand at his favorite spot between two cedar trees in a field along Sugar Hill Road on the Lyons farm. In 1982, Adios Harry passed away at the age of 31. He was buried, spending eternity in his favorite place between those cedar trees. (Courtesy of Rebecca Batson Kidner.)

Lewes resident Hazell Smith, a lifelong horse enthusiast, owned and raced Standardbred horses at Georgetown, Harrington, and Dover Downs Raceways in the 1970s and 1980s. Her love for horses continued into organizing horse shows in the field across the road from her residence on Gills Neck Road. Smith stands in the middle of two horse show participants in the 1960s. (Courtesy of Hazell Smith.)

Georgetown businessman and horseman Nutter Marvel held seasonal carriage drives throughout the Georgetown area on back country roads. Driving the first carriage team is Wayne Wilkins on the left and George Isaacs sitting on the right in a 1970s carriage drive. Nutter Marvel owned several different breeds of carriage horses as well as Standardbred racehorses. (Courtesy of Georgetown Historical Society/Nutter Marvel Museum.)

Two

BRANDYWINE RACEWAY

The history of Brandywine Raceway began on October 15, 1949, when a group of men, represented by John W. Kane from New Castle County, applied for a harness race meet in 1950. The group was told by the local Harness Racing Commission that its application would be considered in the future. In October 1952, the Harness Racing Commission required a payment of $10,000 to build any new tracks in New Castle County, and at that time, Nathan Miller was requested to be at the next meeting. At the next meeting on November 7, 1952, Miller put a $10,000 check into the possession of the commission for the application, license, and fees, and Brandywine's application was approved. On December 3, 1952, all building permits and plans were presented to the commission, with the completion of Brandywine Raceway expected on December 7, 1952 (an extension was granted due to a construction strike). On January 12, 1953, Miller met with the commission, answering questions about how he would acquire the Turner and Talley farms for development into Brandywine Raceway. During the meeting, it was disclosed that Nathan Miller paid for both properties from his own out-of-pocket cash (no financing). At this meeting, BRA, Inc., got its first 20 racing dates set for September 1953. Miller received from the State of Delaware the harness racing franchise license for New Castle County to operate Brandywine Raceway. On September 7, 1953, Brandywine Raceway opened to the unexpected crowd of 16,000 people, surprising Howard and Nathan Miller.

As interest grew and the track needed to expand by the mid-1960s, Howard Miller, as track president, was the driving force behind the renovations. Brandywine's largest ever crowd—25,278—came on a July evening in 1970. Under Howard Miller's leadership, Brandywine had a reputation as one of the fastest and safest racing surfaces in the world. Bill Davies installed a synthetic racing surface during the 1966–1967 renovation, increasing the size of the track to five-eighths of a mile, which was state-of-the-art for its time. As a result, most of the great Standardbreds were raced at Brandywine during its 36-year history. Howard Miller's Brandywine Raceway had more than 100 nights of racing and paid nearly $4 million annually to the State of Delaware from its betting proceeds and hundreds of thousands of dollars more in taxes and other fees.

The year 1953 saw the growth of the "buy now, pay later" mentality with carmakers leading the way by allowing longer periods to pay for a new car. Unions were gaining strength with more workers, and wage and price controls were ending. Unemployment was at 2.9 percent, and increases in the standard of living continued to grow, appearing to have no boundaries. A teacher's average salary was $4,254, and a pound of round steak was 90¢. The first color television sets appeared, selling for $1,175, and transistor radios started sell. These are some of the events that were going on when Nathan Miller decided to take on a monumental task in developing a harness racetrack in the Brandywine Valley of New Castle.

In a September 1958 *Hoof Beats* interview, Howard Miller, president of Brandywine, claimed that he was at the track early in the morning and closed the day well after the last race finished, which is when he made himself available for closing comments to the press and business officials. After clearing up mountains of administrative duties, he found the time every day to visit behind the scenes in the barn area and keep his finger on the horsemen's pulse. His concern for their welfare was genuine. What may seem like a pleasant chat with a horseman or a groom may be just that, but then again, it was an opportunity for them to unload any problems or complaints they may have had. The chance that something would be done about it was better than on an odds-on favorite. Miller's policies towards horsemen, employees, and fans at Brandywine were not passive ones. He continued to find ways to make them content with the conditions at the raceway. (Courtesy of Michael Wirtschafter.)

The construction crew is pictured in 1953, erecting the grandstand metal framing while engineers and Nathan Miller (pictured in his 70s, at far right) look over the site. After completion of the facility, Miller observed his plans for one of the nation's leading harness tracks bloom under the direction of his son Howard Miller. (Courtesy of Michael Wirtschafter.)

Brandywine Raceway, or the "Big B" as it was nicknamed, was completed with a half-mile track, grandstand, stables, paddocks, and opened for its first race on September 7, 1953, before a spectacular crowd of 16,000 people. (Courtesy of Michael Wirtschafter.)

Brandywine Raceway was completed at a cost of $2,295,000 (including the land) in September 1953, and this aerial view shows a remarkable facility. Many of the sport's equine stars were born or made an appearance at the Big B, and plenty of the Grand Circuit trainers were stabled at Brandywine. The Battle of the Brandywine was originally contested there. (Courtesy of Michael Wirtschafter.)

To Howard and Nathan Miller's surprise, 16,000 people arrived on opening night at Brandywine Raceway on September 7, 1953. Pacer Head Pin won the first race with J. Wilcutts in the bike. E. Cobb would win the 1953 season, leading driving honors in 51 starts with 10 wins, nine seconds, and five thirds. (Courtesy of Michael Wirtschafter.)

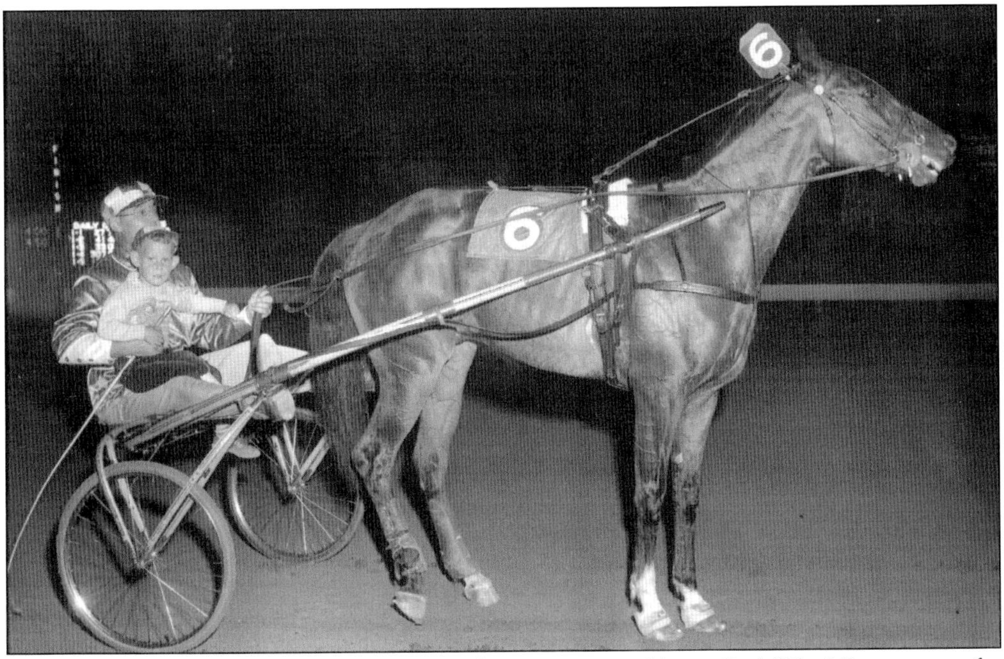

Driver and owner George Brenneman takes his seven-year-old son Carl "Flip" Brenneman for a ride back to the paddock with trotter Hoot Dolmont after a win at Brandywine in 1956. Carl "Flip" Brenneman would later follow his father's footsteps into a career in horse racing. (Courtesy of Vicky Brenneman.)

Covered with mud, driver and owner George Brenneman, piloting Burbank Wyn, finds his way through horse traffic to go on and win at Brandywine Raceway in 1957. Burbank Wyn continued to win several times for the Brenneman stables for the next seven years at Delaware, Maryland, and New York racetracks. (Courtesy of Vicky Brenneman.)

Brandywine Raceway president Howard Miller is standing on the right of winning driver C. Martin in the victory lane with horse Grand R. Volo after the No. 8 race at Brandywine Raceway on August 2, 1957. (Courtesy of Michael Wirtschafter.)

After managing his oil delivery business during the day, horseman Nutter Marvel would travel to the Delaware racetracks to watch his horse race. Nutter Marvel, standing on the far right in the winner's circle at Brandywine Raceway, is pictured with his racehorse Widow Woman in the early 1960s. (Courtesy of Georgetown Historical Society/Nutter Marvel Museum.)

Young Brenda Lewis Bramble holds her grandfather Gardner Bryan's horse Success Guy in the winner's circle at Brandywine Raceway on September 5, 1960. Brenda Lewis Bramble would continue a career in the racing industry, operating a racing stable and volunteering her time as the vice president of the Delaware Standardbred Owners Association (DSOA). (Courtesy of Brenda Lewis Bramble.)

Late in the evening, horses pacing down the stretch, Laurel horseman Gardner Bryan's Success Guy pulls out in front to narrowly win at Brandywine Raceway in 2:06.2 time with driver Allen Myer in the bike on September 5, 1960. Allen Myer won the 1960 season-leading driver in 136 starts with 25 wins, 20 seconds, and 14 thirds. (Courtesy of Brenda Lewis Bramble.)

Winner's circle regular Widow Woman paced to another win in 2:07 with W. Savage in the bike and Nutter Marvel standing third from the right at Brandywine Raceway on August 10, 1961. (Courtesy of Georgetown Historical Society/Nutter Marvel Museum.)

Pacer Hal Reward, winner of the sixth race on September 11, 1961, finished in 2:03.3 time with driver Charles Fitzpatrick Jr. in the bike at Brandywine Raceway. Pictured (from left to right) are Sen. Curtis Steen, Van Brown, ? Wilgue, Charles Fitzpatrick Jr., John R. Hitchens, Harvey Spicer, Howard Miller, Harvey Lawson, and Nutter Marvel. (Courtesy of Georgetown Historical Society/Nutter Marvel Museum.)

Horses are pictured warming up on a sunny afternoon before the evening race events started at Brandywine Raceway on July 4, 1962. The half-mile track was celebrated as the finest on the East Coast. Some of the area's artists showcased their work at the track, such as N.C. Wyeth, Albert Gold, Larry Johnson, and Marilyn Privitar, who were seen on the track property at various occasions. (Courtesy of Harrington Historical Society.)

The Brandywine Raceway paddock is busy with grooms walking—or cooling out—their racehorses after the race events on July 4, 1962. In the background of the photograph, the water tower used as an additional water resource to supply the massive facility can be seen. (Courtesy of Harrington Historical Society.)

Lusty Dud takes the win in 2:06.4 for owner, trainer, and driver George Brenneman (in the bike) at Brandywine Raceway on July 20, 1964. Howard Miller played a pivotal role in bringing major league harness racing to Delaware at Brandywine Raceway. Miller was a Harvard graduate and held a private law practice in Wilmington from the 1930s to the 1950s. (Courtesy of Vicky Brenneman.)

Another win from the George Brenneman stables as his trotter Sharpie finished the race in 2:08 at Brandywine Raceway on August 5, 1964. Brenneman is pictured in the bike. (Courtesy of Vicky Brenneman.)

W. "Billy" Haughton was a frequent trainer and driver at Brandywine Raceway as well as a visiting resident of the winner's circle on numerous occasions. Owners Mr. and Mrs. Pat Digennaro are pictured with their racehorse Duke Rodney in Brandywine's winner's circle on September 4, 1964. Billy Haughton drove Vicar Hanover, which was partially owned by Howard Miller. (Courtesy of Harrington Historical Society.)

Burbank Wyn was still going strong in 1964, dueling out down the stretch for the win in 2:04.2 on July 22 with owner, trainer, and driver George Brenneman in the bike at Brandywine Raceway. People from all over the East Coast—such as fans, owners, trainers, and drivers from the Meadowlands, Yonkers, and Freehold—would make the three-and-a-half hour trip to go to the Big B several times a year. (Courtesy of Vicky Brenneman.)

Legendary trainer and driver Stanley Dancer frequently drove racehorses at Brandywine Raceway throughout the 1960s and 1970s. This photograph shows Stanley Dancer driving an unidentified horse to the winner's circle at Brandywine in 1963. (Courtesy of Michael Wirtschafter.)

It happens occasionally when a horse race results in a dead heat, and that is exactly what happened between Sharon News and Eunice Gold on July 26, 1966, at Brandywine Raceway. They both finished with the time of 2:07.1 for trainers and drivers George Brenneman and J. Wilcutts and owners Yahudas Stable and Joseph E. Palmer. (Courtesy of Vicky Brenneman.)

Legendary driving sensation Herve Filion holds the all-time record for the most career wins in North America with over 15,000. On August 16, 1966, trainer and driver Filion pilots trotter Mr. Lew into the winner's circle, finishing with the time of 2:09 for owner Fluer De Lys Stables at Brandywine Raceway. (Courtesy of Harrington Historical Society.)

Howard Miller (second from the left) would make frequent visits to the winner's circle with friends and acquaintances. In this photograph, Miller is celebrating in the winner's circle at Brandywine Raceway with unidentified owners and driver Billy Haughton in the 1960s. (Courtesy of Michael Wirtschafter.)

Taking a break from his administrative duties as president of Brandywine Raceway, Howard Miller (third from left) and Dave Herman (second from left) walk among the stables, paying frequent visits with the area horsemen throughout Brandywine's facilities in the 1960s. (Courtesy of Michael Wirtschafter.)

Pictured is a July 30, 1972, Brandywine Raceway program signed by Duke Ellington. Brandywine Raceway featured celebrities and bands in the clubhouse. On this date, Ellington and his orchestra were playing at the Big B. One of the greats, Bret Hanover, won his 47th race in 50 career starts at Brandywine in 1966. (Courtesy of Michael Wirtschafter.)

At the close of the 1966 season, Brandywine Raceway began a $4-million renovation project with a new, five-eighths mile Bill Davies synthetic surface racetrack; a clubhouse designed by well-known New York architect Lionel Levy; expanded stables; and a parking area, which could accommodate a crowd of 30,000. The entire facility was also landscaped with an infield fountain lake. (Courtesy of Michael Wirtschafter.)

Brandywine Raceway opened its 1967 season with an overflowing crowd at the betting windows. Escalators, stairs, and an elevator were available for people going to the mezzanine level of the glass-enclosed clubhouse, which has two levels of wagering. (Courtesy of Michael Wirtschafter.)

In 1964, Billy Haughton drove Vicar Hanover at Brandywine Raceway, the horse partially owned by Howard and Henny Miller. The Big B's grand renovation, completed in 1967, sparkled in the evening sky and illuminated its image in the infield fountain lake. Nathan and Howard Miller could be justifiably proud of their accomplished endeavor in the magnificent structure. (Courtesy of Michael Wirtschafter.)

Delaware governor Charles L. Terry Jr. attended the Brandywine Raceway's Dedication Day on August 3, 1967, and is pictured standing in the new clubhouse dining area, which seats approximately 1,000. The comfortable seats in the front and on the right, facing the track, were for an additional 1,200 spectators, and overall, there was viewing for some 10,000. (Courtesy of Michael Wirtschafter.)

The Millers had an outstanding relationship with owners, trainers, and drivers and were noted for the track's sponsorship of standout promotions, bringing huge crowds to the raceway. During its years of racing, Brandywine began and maintained an outstanding reputation as one of the sport's preeminent facilities. The Millers' focus on racing quality and integrity was carried during all of the track's 36 seasons of operation. (Courtesy of Michael Wirtschafter.)

Governor Terry is addressing Brandywine Raceway's board of directors on Dedication Day, August 3, 1967, in the first-level dining area before the start of the evening races. Brandywine Raceway quickly became the leading nighttime sports entertainment venue in Delaware and one of the top attractions in the Delaware Valley. Brandywine Raceway was instrumental in bringing people to Delaware and settling in the Delaware Valley. (Courtesy of Michael Wirtschafter.)

On August 3, 1967, Brandywine Raceway commemorated a monumental milestone when it officially dedicated its $4-million clubhouse and facility. The magnificent structure, a masterpiece in design, comfort, and convenience, marked a giant step in the track's long-range program of progress and expansion and fulfilled the cherished dreams of Pres. Howard Miller and associates. (Courtesy of Michael Wirtschafter.)

Winner of the fourth race at Brandywine Raceway on August 23, 1973, was trotter Party Manners, pictured with trainer and driver Jesse Whalen in the bike, with the time of 2:07.3 for owner Old Grandads Stable. President and general manager of Brandywine Raceway Howard Miller is pictured second from right. (Courtesy of Michael Wirtschafter.)

Pacer Baron's Boy won the fifth race in 158.3 for trainer R. Moreau, Dr. Michael Guitard, and owner La Ferme Sagbec, Inc., at Brandywine Raceway. Howard Miller is first on the left and would frequent the winner's circle, meeting friends, associates, and strangers. Through the words of those that knew him, "he's a swell guy." (Courtesy of Michael Wirtschafter.)

Trainer, driver, and owner Roman Miller pilots his pacer J. Dominion to a 10th-race finish in 2:05.3 at Brandywine Raceway on May 19, 1978. Miller continued his racing career into his 70s with a string of successful horses. (Courtesy of Roman Miller.)

World champion of harness racing Eddie Davis, who resides in Delaware, won five leading driver titles at Brandywine Raceway through the 1970s and early 1980s. He also holds several leading driver titles at Dover Downs and Harrington Raceway. (Courtesy of Delaware Historical Society.)

Delaware horseman and driver Eddie Davis is having a discussion with fellow horsemen and drivers in the paddock of Brandywine Raceway in the 1970s. Celebrities would make appearances at Brandywine Raceway, such as Wilt Chamberlin, Julius Irving, Darryl Dawkins, Duke Ellington, and Count Basie, to name a few. Politicians were also a staple at the track, including Gov. Pete Dupont, Sen. Joe Biden, and Sen. Bill Roth. (Courtesy of Delaware Historical Society.)

World champion pacer Direct Scooter, a frequent visitor to the Big B, became the fastest four-year-old in history over an American five-eighths mile track in 1980, posting a 1:54.2 time with driver Warren Cameron in the bike at Brandywine Raceway. In the photograph, Direct Scooter is standing by after a brief warm-up session. (Courtesy of Delaware Historical Society.)

Pacer Direct Scooter is pictured at speed, setting the record at Brandywine Raceway with Warren Cameron in the bike. Direct Scooter was considered to be one of the top free-for-all pacers of all time, winning 36 out of 60 races over his two-year period between 1979 and 1980. Scoring his lifetime mark of 1:54 at Hollywood Park, he was named Aged Pacer of the Year in 1980. (Courtesy of Delaware Historical Society.)

In the late afternoon, with the sun setting in the west, Mr. Regal is leading the first race, coming down the stretch to the finish line and winning in 2:05 for owner Flowing Acres. He started the evening race card at Brandywine Raceway with trainer and driver Austin "Ned" Galentine in the bike on August 2, 1971. (Courtesy of Harrington Historical Society.)

Fighting his way through to the finish line in the first race is pacer Harry P. in 2:05.3, along with trainer and driver Austin "Ned" Galentine in the bike, for owner Flowing Acres at Brandywine Raceway on June 30, 1974. (Courtesy of Harrington Historical Society.)

Trainer and driver Walter Marks drives pacer Rebel Heel for a win in the second race, finishing 2:06.1 on August 22, 1972, at Brandywine Raceway while owner Hazell Smith (on the right) joins the celebration in the winner's circle. Smith, a lifelong horse enthusiast, still resides on her horse farm in Lewes. (Courtesy of Hazell Smith.)

Pacer Rebel Heel, owned by Lewes resident Hazell Smith, takes the race to an easy win on August 22, 1972, at Brandywine Raceway in 2:06.1 on a clear evening in New Castle County with trainer and driver Walter Marks in the bike. (Courtesy of Hazell Smith.)

Pacer Ginny Jo Diamond is racing to a win at Brandywine Raceway on May 16, 1973, for owner Melvin Joseph of Georgetown. Trainer and driver William Savage, in the bike, drove Ginny Jo Diamond with a time of 2:03.4. Ginny Jo Diamond was named after Melvin Joseph's children, Virginia and Joe Ann. (Courtesy of Joe Ann Adams.)

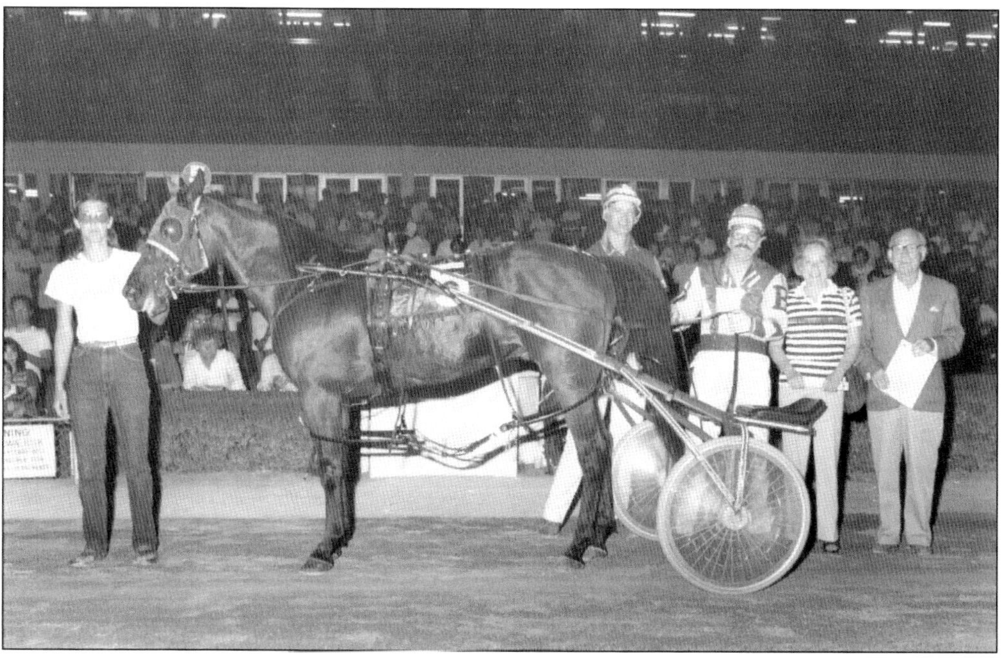

Pacer Star Beau pulls out a win in 158.4 for owner Old Grandads Stable. Trainer Richard Jensen and driver Sam Belote (holding the reins) are pictured on July 10, 1983, at Brandywine Raceway. In the photograph, Howard Miller is on the far right, joining the festive occasion in the winner's circle. (Courtesy of Michael Wirtschafter.)

Horseman, farmer, and owner Wayne Wilkins (on the right) celebrates in the winner's circle at Brandywine Raceway with his pacer Hoe Down on July 11, 1979, after finishing in 2:02.2 with trainer and driver Harold Frazier in the bike. Wayne Wilkins is a relative of Charles H. Wilkins, who created Georgetown Raceway in the 1930s. (Courtesy of Wayne Wilkins.)

Two-year-old trotter Cooper Lobell wins the "George Wilkes," finishing in 2:04 for owner Messinger Stables. Lobell was trained by J. Johnson and driven by Ray Tripp at Brandywine Raceway on June 10, 1981, in the early evening. (Courtesy of Michael Wirtschafter.)

In 1980, Brandywine was rated the fastest five-eighths mile track in North America. A c. 1970s photograph shows the racehorses going to the gate car in preparation before launching off at the starting line. Brandywine had drivers like Eddie Cobb, Ross Hayter, and Jimmy Larente, who were regulars, and horses like Town Drunk, Albatross, Nihilator, Vicar Hanover, Adios Butler, and Niatross. (Courtesy of Harrington Historical Society.)

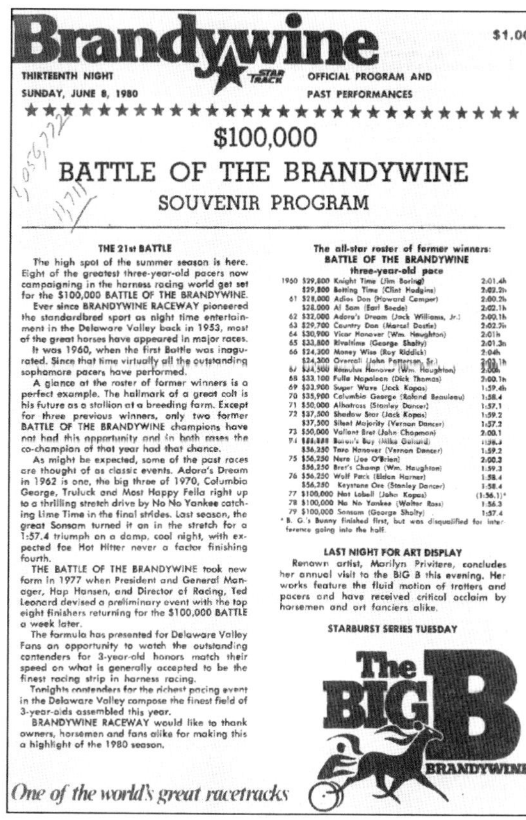

Brandywine $1.00

THIRTEENTH NIGHT
SUNDAY, JUNE 8, 1980

OFFICIAL PROGRAM AND
PAST PERFORMANCES

$100,000
BATTLE OF THE BRANDYWINE
SOUVENIR PROGRAM

THE 21st BATTLE

The high spot of the summer season is here. Eight of the greatest three-year-old pacers now campaigning in the harness racing world get set for the $100,000 BATTLE OF THE BRANDYWINE.

Ever since BRANDYWINE RACEWAY pioneered the standardbred sport as night time entertainment in the Delaware Valley back in 1953, most of the great horses have appeared in major races.

It was 1960, when the first Battle was inaugurated. Since that time virtually all the outstanding sophomore pacers have performed.

A glance at the roster of former winners is a perfect example. The hallmark of a great colt is his future as a stallion at a breeding farm. Except for three previous winners, only two former BATTLE OF THE BRANDYWINE champions have not had this opportunity and in both cases the co-champion of that year had that chance.

As might be expected, some of the past races are thought of as classic events. Adora's Dream in 1962 is one, the big three of 1970, Columbia George, Truluck and Most Happy Fella right up to a thrilling stretch drive by No No Yankee catching Lime Time in the final strides. Last season, the great Sonsam turned it on in the stretch for a 1:57.4 triumph on a damp, cool night, with expected foe Hot Hitter never a factor finishing fourth.

THE BATTLE OF THE BRANDYWINE took new form in 1977 when President and General Manager, Hap Hansen, and Director of Racing, Ted Leonard devised a preliminary event with the top eight finishers returning for the $100,000 BATTLE a week later.

The formula has presented for Delaware Valley Fans an opportunity to watch the outstanding contenders for 3-year-old honors match their speed on what is generally accepted to be the finest racing strip in harness racing.

Tonights contenders for the richest pacing event in the Delaware Valley compose the finest field of 3-year-olds assembled this year.

BRANDYWINE RACEWAY would like to thank owners, horsemen and fans alike for making this a highlight of the 1980 season.

The all-star roster of former winners:
BATTLE OF THE BRANDYWINE
three-year-old pace

1960	$29,800	Knight Time (Jim Boring)	2:01.4h
	$29,800	Betting Time (Clint Hodgins)	2:02.2h
61	$28,000	Adios Don (Howard Camper)	2:00.2h
	$28,000	Al Sam (Earl Beede)	2:02.1h
62	$32,000	Adora's Dream (Jack Williams, Jr.)	2:00.1h
63	$29,700	Country Don (Marcel Dostie)	2:02.2h
64	$30,900	Vicar Hanover (Wm. Haughton)	2:01h
65	$33,800	Rivaltime (George Sholty)	2:01.3h
66	$24,300	Money Wise (Roy Riddick)	2:04h
	$24,300	Overcall (John Patterson, Sr.)	[illegible]
67	$24,500	Romulus Hanover (Wm. Haughton)	2:00h
68	$33,100	Fulla Napoleon (Dick Thomas)	2:00.1h
69	$33,900	Super Wave (Jack Kopas)	1:59.4h
70	$35,900	Columbia George (Roland Beaulieu)	1:58.4
71	$50,000	Albatross (Stanley Dancer)	1:57.1
72	$37,500	Shadow Star (Jack Kopas)	1:59.2
	$37,500	Silent Majority (Vernon Dancer)	1:57.2
73	$50,000	Valiant Bret (John Chapman)	2:00.1
74	[illegible]	[illegible]	[illegible]
	$56,250	Taro Hanover (Vernon Dancer)	1:59.2
75	$56,250	Nero (Joe O'Brien)	2:00.3
	$56,250	Bret's Champ (Wm. Haughton)	1:59.3
76	$56,250	Wolf Pack (Eldon Harner)	1:58.4
	$56,250	Keystone Ore (Stanley Dancer)	1:58.4
77	$100,000	Hot Lobell (John Kopas)	(1:56.1)*
78	$100,000	No No Yankee (Walter Ross)	1:56.3
79	$100,000	Sonsam (George Sholty)	1:57.4

* B. G.'s Bunny finished first, but was disqualified for interference going into the half.

LAST NIGHT FOR ART DISPLAY

Renown artist, Marilyn Privitere, concludes her annual visit to the BIG B this evening. Her works feature the fluid motion of trotters and pacers and have received critical acclaim by horsemen and art fanciers alike.

STARBURST SERIES TUESDAY

The BIG B BRANDYWINE

One of the world's great racetracks

The Battle of the Brandywine was a yearly premier event that brought the best horses from all over North America together to battle it out for the supreme title. A June 8, 1980, Brandywine Raceway program, which belonged to president and general manager Howard Miller, shows on the cover and inside the program where he would write down his race notes. (Courtesy of Michael Wirtschafter.)

STARS OF THE 1980 BATTLE

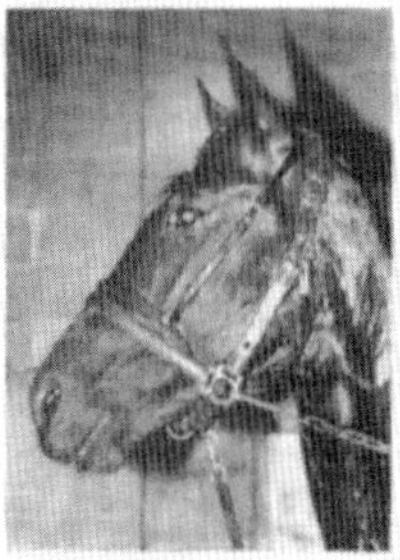

FINIAN HANOVER, p, 3, 2:00.4f

The dark horse of this year's Battle is FINIAN HANOVER. The Tar Heel colt has worked his way through the ranks in the Delaware Valley, from maiden to testing the best three year olds. The Lenore Stables and the Delco Stables own this fast campaigner.

MIKE IZZO has proven himself a solid horseman during his brief career. Brandywine fans frequently see his orange and green silks in the winner's circle behind the likes of Bret's Battle and Davezzo Hanover.

MIKE IZZO

ALBA TIME, p, 3, 1:58.2f

Not many 3 years olds have gone 1:58.2 in May, but that's what ALBA TIME did in winning a Pennsylvania Sires Stake at the Meadows. The Albatross colt has tested the best throughout his career, and has won almost $50,000 for the powerful Barr M Stable of Canada.

JIM MILLER has developed into one of the first-rate Grand Circuit horsemen over the last few years. Driving mostly for owner Melvin Barr, Jim has developed such champions as Tijuana Taxi, Brisco Hanover, and this year's Battle entrant, Alba Time.

JIM MILLER

MUCKALEE STRIKE, p, 2, 1:58.4f

MUCKALEE STRIKE developed powerfully at the end of last season, winning a division of Roosevelt's Silver Spoon Series and just missing in a Grand Circuit Stake at Lexington. This year he has already won in 1:59 here at Brandywine. The Strikt Out colt has won almost $50,000 for Lawrence Kadish of New York.

BILLY HERMAN is no stranger to Grand Circuit competition, having worked for the George Sholty Stable and the Hanover Shoe Farm Stable. Noble Rogue, Hazel Hanover, Boyden Hanover, and Texas, champions all, are but a few of the horses to have benefitted from the services of the Ohio native.

BILL HERMAN

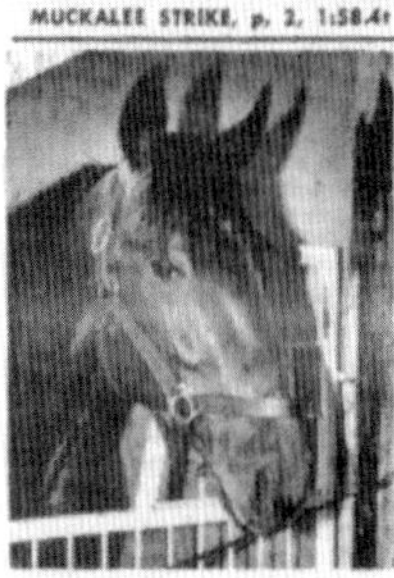

Going into last week's Battle Preview, no one was quite sure how good TRENTON TIME was. The Race Time colt quickly proved himself, winning in a personal best 1:57.1. The D.D.M. Stable-owned colt has also won stakes this year at Roosevelt and Pompano Park, winning over $65,000 in 1980.

Hall of Famer BILLY HAUGHTON has won every major stake in his career, some many times. Billy has won the Battle of the Brandywine three times, with Vicar Hanover, Romulus Hanover and Bret's Champ. Going in 1980, he had won over 4,000 races and over $28 million in purses.

Within the June 8, 1980 program, horse and driver information of the entries for the 1980 Battle of the Brandywine include renowned Billy Haughton, an American harness trainer and driver who held the most record-winning drives of his time. A native of Gloversville, New York, Haughton grew up on a farm, where he competed in fairground races, sharpening his skills as a harness driver. A career record of 4,910 wins—roughly $40 million in revenues—he held a career first in annual winnings 12 times in 1952–1959, 1963, 1965, 1967, and 1968. Haughton was one of three drivers to win the Hambletonian four times, the only driver to win the Little Brown Jug five times, and the only driver to win the Messenger Stakes seven times. Haughton perished in a racing accident from severe head injuries at Yonkers Raceway in Valhalla, New York. (Courtesy of Michael Wirtschafter.)

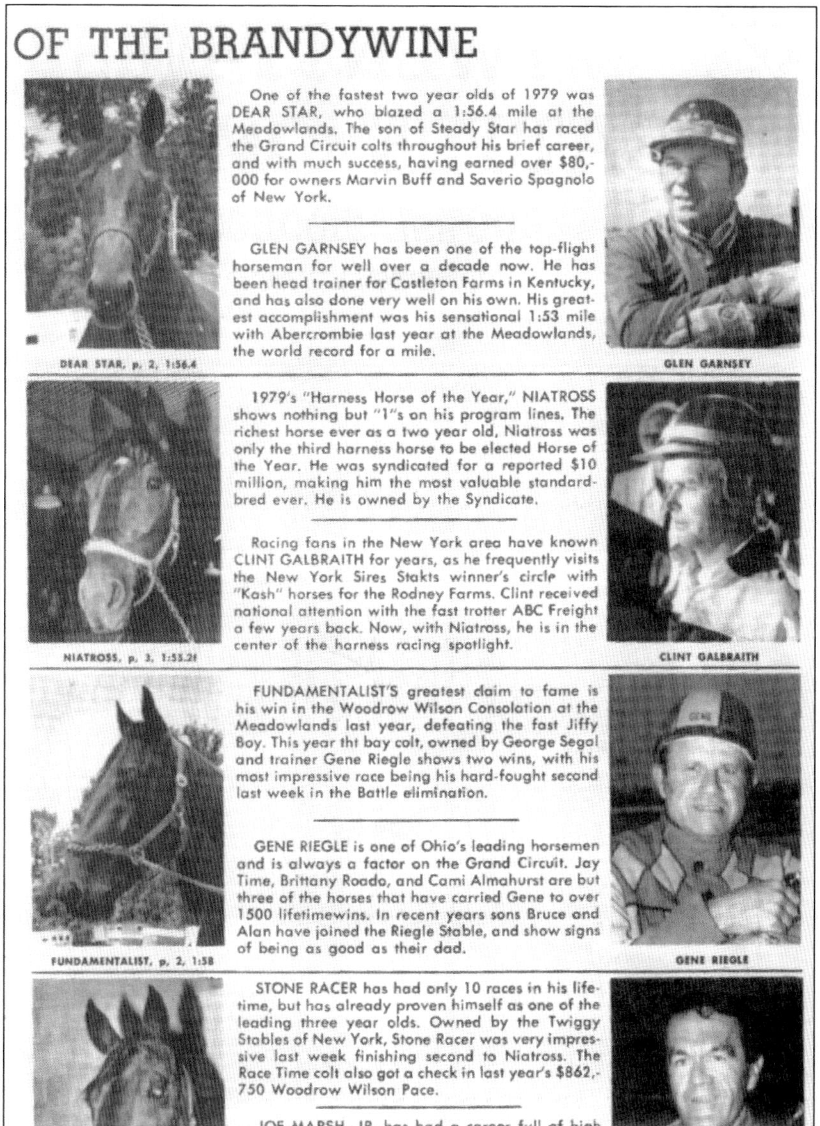

OF THE BRANDYWINE

DEAR STAR, p. 2, 1:56.4

One of the fastest two year olds of 1979 was DEAR STAR, who blazed a 1:56.4 mile at the Meadowlands. The son of Steady Star has raced the Grand Circuit colts throughout his brief career, and with much success, having earned over $80,-000 for owners Marvin Buff and Saverio Spagnolo of New York.

GLEN GARNSEY has been one of the top-flight horseman for well over a decade now. He has been head trainer for Castleton Farms in Kentucky, and has also done very well on his own. His greatest accomplishment was his sensational 1:53 mile with Abercrombie last year at the Meadowlands, the world record for a mile.

GLEN GARNSEY

NIATROSS, p. 3, 1:55.2f

1979's "Harness Horse of the Year," NIATROSS shows nothing but "1"s on his program lines. The richest horse ever as a two year old, Niatross was only the third harness horse to be elected Horse of the Year. He was syndicated for a reported $10 million, making him the most valuable standardbred ever. He is owned by the Syndicate.

Racing fans in the New York area have known CLINT GALBRAITH for years, as he frequently visits the New York Sires Stakts winner's circle with "Kash" horses for the Rodney Farms. Clint received national attention with the fast trotter ABC Freight a few years back. Now, with Niatross, he is in the center of the harness racing spotlight.

CLINT GALBRAITH

FUNDAMENTALIST, p. 2, 1:58

FUNDAMENTALIST'S greatest claim to fame is his win in the Woodrow Wilson Consolation at the Meadowlands last year, defeating the fast Jiffy Boy. This year tht bay colt, owned by George Segal and trainer Gene Riegle shows two wins, with his most impressive race being his hard-fought second last week in the Battle elimination.

GENE RIEGLE is one of Ohio's leading horsemen and is always a factor on the Grand Circuit. Jay Time, Brittany Roado, and Cami Almahurst are but three of the horses that have carried Gene to over 1500 lifetimewins. In recent years sons Bruce and Alan have joined the Riegle Stable, and show signs of being as good as their dad.

GENE RIEGLE

STONE RACER, p. 3, 2:02.3h

STONE RACER has had only 10 races in his lifetime, but has already proven himself as one of the leading three year olds. Owned by the Twiggy Stables of New York, Stone Racer was very impressive last week finishing second to Niatross. The Race Time colt also got a check in last year's $862,-750 Woodrow Wilson Pace.

JOE MARSH, JR. has had a career full of high points and great achievements. He has won numerous driving championships in Chicago, and is 12th lifetime in purse earnings. He has driven such stars as Carelee Time, Young Quinn, and Stone Racer, his horse in this year's Battle. But Marsh's greatest accomplishment was winning the 1974 World Driving Championship against the cream of the world's driving stars.

JOE MARSH, JR.

The second page of the same program for the Battle of the Brandywine shows world champion racehorse Niatross. Niatross won the Triple Crown of Harness Racing for Pacers as well as the Meadowlands Pace, which was the first $1-million race for either Thoroughbred or Standardbred racing history, in 1980. In Lexington, Kentucky, at the "Red Mile" during a time trial, Niatross beat the world record by three seconds, placing a mark of 1:49.1. In 1981, by the time Niatross was retired to stud at Castleton Farm, he had won 37 out of 39 races during his racing career, made more money than any other Standardbred in history, and demanded a high price for his stud fees. Niatross earned Horse of the Year for 1979 and 1980, Harness Horse of the Decade for the 1980s, and New York Post Athlete of the Year for 1980. (Courtesy of Michael Wirtschafter.)

Elsie Bulter won the sixth race, "The Starlet," for owner Melvin Joseph with a finish of 2:00.1 with trainer and driver J.D. Dennis at Brandywine Raceway on June 14, 1980. A friend of Joseph (second on the right) is Al Unser, the legendary race car driver. (Courtesy of Joe Ann Adams.)

Georgetown businessman and horseman Melvin Joseph (fourth from the right) visits the winner's circle at Brandywine Raceway on September 4, 1982. Pictured is the horse that bears the name of his favorite number, Mr. Forty Nine, who won in 1:57.2 with driver Presley Moore Jr. in the bike for trainer D. Shockley. (Courtesy of Joe Ann Adams.)

Three

Georgetown Raceway

Georgetown Raceway–Delmarva Raceway is located on US Route 9, east of Georgetown, Delaware. It dates back to the early 1930s, when times were hard and entertainment was what a person created. Horse racing was everyone's form of entertainment, commanding thousands of patrons to fill the grandstand in the days when there was not much of anything else other than work. People dressed up in their best attire for a well-deserved weekend night out on the town.

In 1917, Charles H. Wilkins purchased a farm near Georgetown for $3,975, and in the early 1930s, he, a timberman by trade, cut the timber off his 70-acre farm and created a half-mile oval racetrack with a mule and plow in the field north of US Route 9. Timber cut from the farm was used to build the wooden grandstand, box seats, and a concession stand.

At the time, the Delmarva Raceway was one of the first racetracks in the country to install pole lights for nighttime racing. In the late 1940s, along with horse racing, Charles and his son Elwood "Boots" Wilkins promoted rodeos, horse shows, and auto racing to fill the need for entertainment and excitement for local residents. Barn paddocks were provided for the area horsemen behind the Wilkins residence. In 1952, Charles sold the racetrack for $20,000 to a group of local investors, including area businessman and horseman Nutter Marvel (president of Del-Mar-Va, Inc.), who applied for United States Trotting Association–sanctioned race dates to operate a racehorse meet.

From 1953 to 1964, when horse race matinees were scheduled on Saturday afternoons, thousands of people would fill the wooden grandstand from as far away as New Jersey, crossing the Lewes Ferry. In 1964, Georgetown Raceway was sold again to another set of investors, including Melvin Joseph, who began to make big plans for the raceway, obtaining USTA–sanctioned race dates for scheduled pari-mutuel horse racing. These investors purchased 30 acres from Marshal Wilkins for an aggressive expansion, building parking lots, a new racetrack surface, a new closed-in grandstand for wintertime racing, and new paddocks and stables. Georgetown Raceway operated pari-mutuel racing from 1965 to 1972.

In 2009, there was some speculation that Georgetown Raceway, now called Georgetown Downs, may be revived in the future.

In the 1930s, Boots Wilkins would travel with his father to Philadelphia to buy horses and mules for timbering. The horses were shipped by boat down the Delaware Bay and up the Murderkill River to Frederica, where Boots would meet them and walk them to Georgetown. Boots used his father's workhorses and mules to carve out a racetrack. Pictured is an unidentified horse and driver at Charles H. Wilkins's racetrack in 1945. (Courtesy of Wayne Wilkins.)

Racehorses come off the starting gate truck at the Charles H. and Boots Wilkins Raceway (also called Delmarva Raceway) in Georgetown in 1949. In the early days, Boots and his wife sold hot dogs and soft drinks to help raise the $50 purses while Mabel Wilkins, Boots Wilkins's sister, collected 50¢ admission at the gate. (Courtesy of Eddie Lambden.)

Boots Wilkins (right) prepares his horse for the feature race in the paddock area at Delmarva Raceway with his driver Elmer (left) in 1946. During its early years, the racetrack often failed to collect enough money at the gate from entries to pay the winner's purses, and Boots's father would pay them out of his pocket. (Courtesy of Eddie Lambden.)

Saturday afternoons at the Wilkins Farm became racing day, and families would arrive by car or farm wagon, sometimes bringing along picnic lunches and making a day of it. An unidentified couple washes their horse in the paddock area after a race at Wilkins Farm's racetrack, Delmarva Raceway. (Courtesy of Georgetown Historical Society/Nutter Marvel Museum.)

Boots Wilkins's racetrack served double duty in the 1940s and 1950s as a stock car track. At first, spectators lined the fence around the track, sometimes bringing their own chairs. Later, Boots built a wooden grandstand with timber from his farm, and the Georgetown racetrack became the focal point of weekend entertainment. Melvin Joseph's No. 49 is driven by "Flying Dutchman" Johnny Stoltzfus. (Courtesy of Joe Ann Adams.)

In 1952, local Georgetown oil businessman and horseman Nutter Marvel (pictured) and a group of investors, including Del-Mar-Va Inc., purchased Charles and Boots Wilkins's racetrack for $20,000. Delmarva Raceway operated scheduled horse race matinees from 1953 to 1964. (Courtesy of Georgetown Historical Society/Nutter Marvel Museum.)

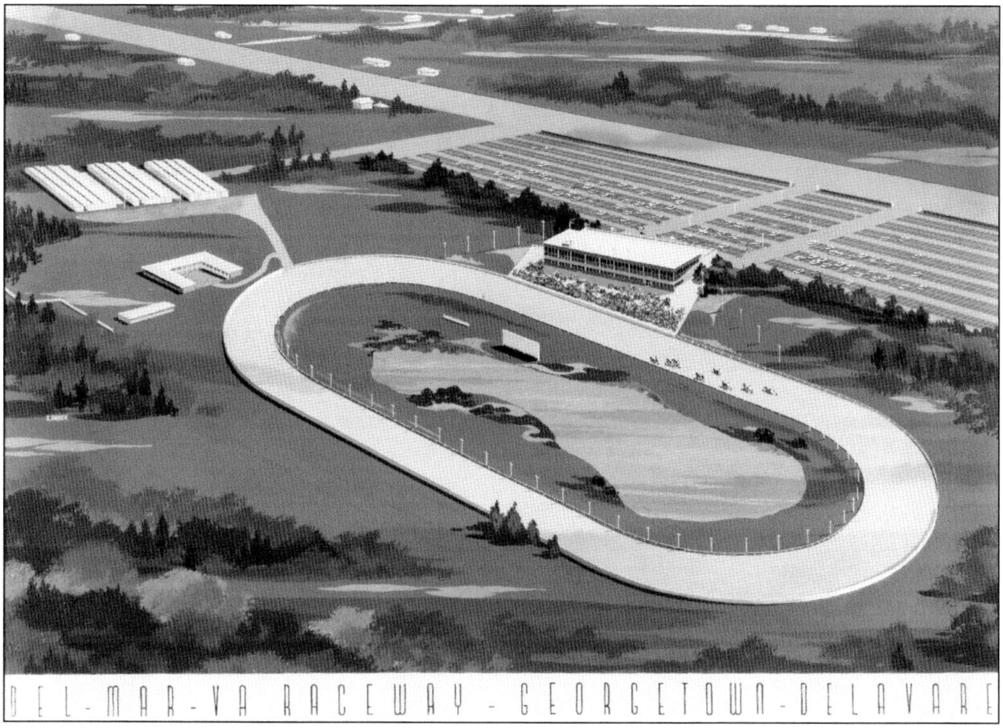

In 1964, Delmarva Raceway was purchased by another set of investors, including Georgetown construction businessman and horseman Melvin Joseph, who had big plans to expand and renovate the facility using the engineered sketch above. (Courtesy of Joe Ann Adams.)

Work began in 1965 at Georgetown Raceway with Melvin Joseph Construction providing the equipment to build a new racing surface. Thirty more acres, located northeast of the facility, were purchased from Marshall Wilkins for an aggressive expansion. Joseph is first on the left, watching the site work begin. (Courtesy of Joe Ann Adams.)

Melvin Joseph's construction crews began work on Georgetown Raceway's racetrack surface and prepared groundwork for new paddocks and barns in 1965. Work continued anxiously and diligently through 1965 with the collaborated efforts of hundreds of personnel associated with the project. (Courtesy of Joe Ann Adams.)

It would take several months of hard work to construct a grandstand, barns, paddocks, and a new parking lot in order to complete the project before its scheduled grand opening race date on Wednesday, November 3, 1965. (Courtesy of Joe Ann Adams.)

Georgetown Raceway, completed in 1965, closely resembles the engineered sketch that was the blueprint for the massive facility. The closed-in grandstand was engineered for the winter months' racing schedule. (Courtesy of Joe Ann Adams.)

Horseman and Georgetown businessman Nutter Marvel drives his racehorse Widow Woman on Georgetown Raceway's new racetrack surface in 1965. Georgetown Raceway sold public stock shares, which Marvel and several Georgetown residents purchased. (Courtesy of Georgetown Historical Society/Nutter Marvel Museum.)

Melvin Joseph (third from the left) stands next to Nutter Marvel, who is holding his horse Widow Woman, with fellow associates of the raceway in 1965. In the photograph, the grandstand is not quite finished; however, the track service has been completed. (Courtesy of Georgetown Historical Society/Nutter Marvel Museum.)

IN DEEP APPRECIATION

Speaking for myself, the officers and directors of Georgetown Racing, Inc., I want to take this opportunity to publicly express the deep appreciation that all of us here at Georgetown Raceway, and particularly myself have for the assistance, encouragement and cooperation to those who made the going over the rough road of the past two years possible, and our dream of this race track a reality.

Two of Delaware's outstanding individuals, Nutter D. Marvel, Georgetown, first horseman of Sussex County, breeder, owner, trainer, director of the U. S. Trotting Association, and true sportsman; and Daniel G. Conant, Rehoboth Beach, former Steward of the Delaware Harness Racing Commission, and all-around horseman, gave of their time and energy to bring back harness racing to Sussex County as a member of trotting's front ranks.

To the Delaware Harness Racing Commission, Joseph R. Pittard, chairman; Claude A. Brittingham, Hudson E. Gruwell and J. Ewell Calhoun, secretary, I am deeply aware of what their cooperation, counsel and guidance have meant to myself and associates, and to the furtherance of the best interests of the track and the sport of harness racing.

To all harness horse fans and lovers of horses of all breeds, we extend the heartiest of welcomes, and invite you to enjoy our sport of trotting through to December 31st.

Cordially,
Edward H. Griffiths,
President

A column in the first program on grand opening day, November 3, 1965, at Georgetown Raceway shows appreciation for the people who helped make the racetrack a reality. Many of the horses that raced at Georgetown Raceway came from Doulby Standardbred Breeding Farm in Georgetown throughout the 1950s and 1960s, which produced foals from more than 100 mares and had at any one time 10 stud horses. (Courtesy of Eddie Lambden.)

Georgetown Raceway opened on Wednesday, November 3, 1965, for a 40-race, pari-mutuel meet, selling race programs for 40¢. It would not be long before George Brenneman's four-year-old Lusty Dud would establish a track record in 2:03.2. There were several more to follow in the raceway's inaugural fall-winter meet. (Courtesy of Eddie Lambden.)

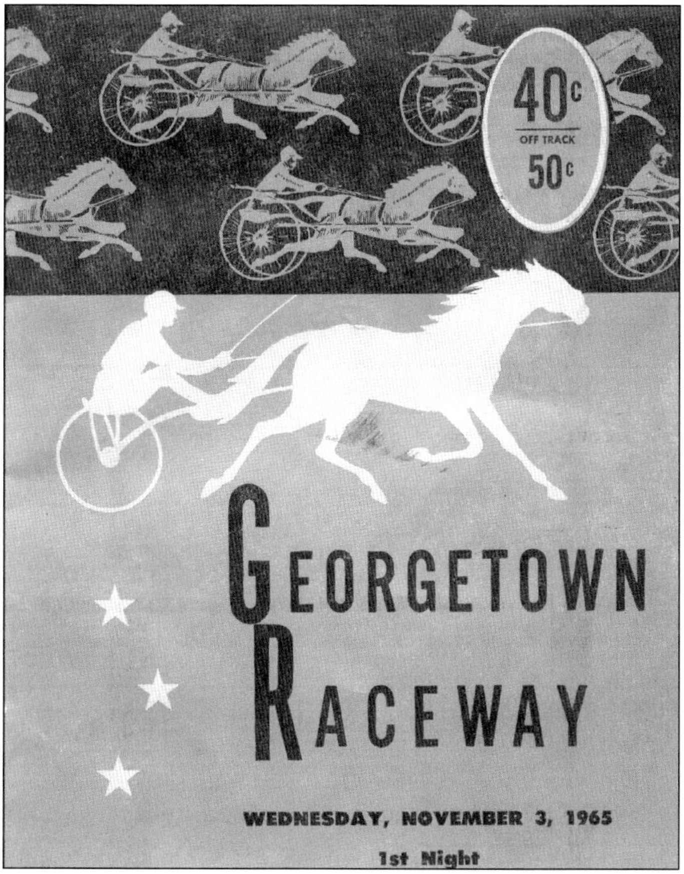

The winner of the fourth race was trotter Capitol Gain in 2:10.2 with driver W. Warrington in the bike. Owners Edward and Aaron Cohan and ? Forman celebrate on the racetrack on November 6, 1965, at Georgetown Raceway. (Courtesy of Eddie Lambden.)

Trainer and driver Elmer Looney (Heather Moffett's grandfather) stands by his racehorse in preparation for the upcoming race at the Georgetown Raceway winter meet in the late 1960s. Heather Moffett is a harness-racing television personality from Harrington, Delaware, and the current host and producer of *Post Time*. (Courtesy of Heather Moffett.)

Nutter Marvel (far right) is pictured in the winner's circle with the winner of the seventh race, Mitzy Hanover, finishing in 2:05.5 with J. Simpson in the bike. Richie Ashburn of the Philadelphia Phillies joins the celebration. (Courtesy of Georgetown Historical Society/ Nutter Marvel Museum.)

Mabel Lambden (sister to Boots Wilkins, one of the original founders of the raceway) stands with a group of Georgetown Raceway associates in front of the harness racing officials' office in 1965. As a young lady, Mabel used to work side by side with her father and brother at the same racing facility in the 1930s and 1940s. (Courtesy of Eddie Lambden.)

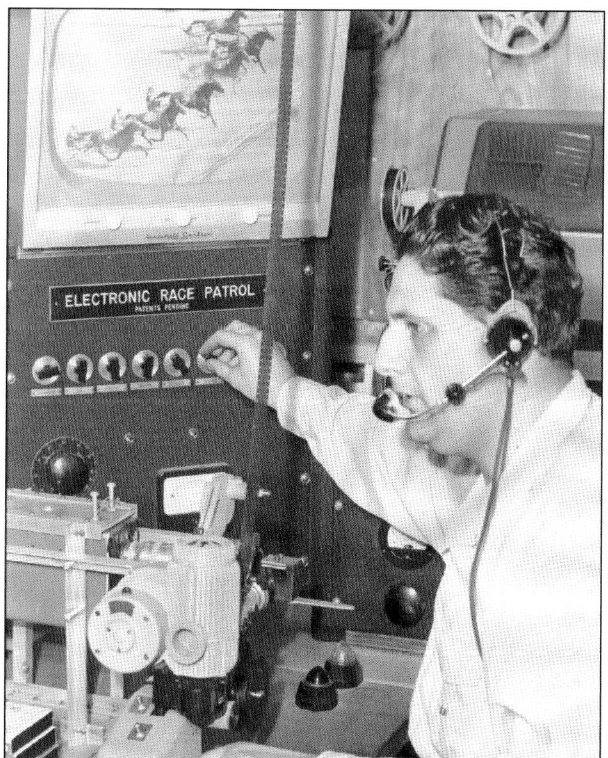

Electronic equipment and television monitors allowed race judges to review instant replays of close finishes and live views of the racetrack. In this photograph, an unidentified person is managing the controls at Georgetown Raceway in the late 1960s. (Courtesy of Georgetown Historical Society/ Nutter Marvel Museum.)

Mr. Newport visits the winner's circle at Georgetown Raceway after the fourth race on December 15, 1965, during the fall-winter meet. Driven by owner and trainer Elmer Looney, Mr. Newport finished in 2:09.3. Looney operated a successful training stable in Viola and campaigned at racetracks throughout Delaware. (Courtesy of Heather Moffett.)

GEORGETOWN RACING ASSOCIATION

Licensed for 1965 by the Delaware State Harness Racing Commission

DELAWARE HARNESS RACING COMMISSION

Joseph R. Pittard	Chairman
Claude A. Brittingham	Member
Hudson E. Gruwell	Member
J. Ewell Calhoun	Executive Secretary
Josh Bennett	Steward
Harold H. Keller	Auditor

RACING OFFICIALS

John E. Ducharme	Presiding Judge
Fred B. Greenley, Jr.	Associate Judge
Cecil Wheatley	Associate Judge
Charles O'Neal	Patrol Judge
John E. Walters	Patrol Judge
Irwin Murray	Patrol Judge
Elmer K. Swan	Paddock Judge
Crawford Holson	Starting Judge
Dr. James R. West	Veterinarian
John Phillips	Racing Secretary
Rose Hall	Clerk of Course
Nellie Ann Hobbs	Marshal

GEORGETOWN RACING ASSOCIATION OFFICIALS

E. H. Griffiths	President
Robert P. Leacy	Vice President
Paul Roth	Secretary
Edwin T. Keller	Director of Racing

DEPARTMENTS

Victory Lane Publishing Co.	Program
Laurence P. Molloy	Mutuels
Electronic Controls, Inc.	Automatic Timer
James J. Moran	Announcer
District Sports Service, Inc.	Catering
G. H. Henning	Track Physician
Nick Varrato	Track Photographer
American Legion	Ambulance
Eye-In-The-Sky	Photo-Finish
Marcia Dickerson	Program Director

This is the 1965 insert in the racing program for the Georgetown Racing Association. In a later newspaper article, Georgetown Raceway set up a national daily-double payoff record for the 1965 campaign, a record unmatched by any other harness track that year. (Courtesy of Eddie Lambden.)

Sitting on the racing bike in Georgetown Raceway's winner's circle, Mabel Lambden joyfully holds on to an unidentified woman's shoulder while Robert Tunnell (right) stands close by in 1965. The driver and racehorse in the photograph are unidentified. (Courtesy of Eddie Lambden.)

Nutter Marvel (second from the left) stands next to new driving star Bobby Myers at Georgetown Raceway in the late 1960s. Few young reinsmen have come along as Myers. Overnight, he gained the confidence that the profession demands, including getting along with horses of all ages and gait and possessing that "light hand" with the reins that sets a first-class driver apart from others. (Courtesy of Georgetown Historical Society/Nutter Marvel Museum.)

Owner Gardner Bryan holds on to his winning pacer King Bonnie who finished with a time of 1:38 of a three-quarter mile after the second race in the evening of January 6, 1966, with E. White in the bike at Georgetown Raceway. Granddaughter Brenda Lewis Bramble (second from right) and Richard "Dick" Lewis (first on the right) join the celebration. (Courtesy of Brenda Lewis Bramble.)

Pacer High Mite is pictured in 1967 in Georgetown Raceway's winner's circle with young Danny Wilkins, whose father, Wayne Wilkins, is standing inside the raceway fence. Wilkins and his son Danny raced and bred Standardbreds and miniature racehorses until the early 2000s. (Courtesy of Wayne Wilkins.)

Owner, trainer, and driver Wayde Marsh is pictured in the winner's circle at Georgetown Raceway on February 16, 1968, with 14-year-old trotter Royal Rodney, who, as a three-year-old, raced in the Hambletonian at the Meadowlands, placing fourth. (Courtesy of Wayde Marsh.)

Trotter Lord Marc cruised to a finish of 2:09.4 with trainer and driver Charles Marsh in the bike. Owner Hazell Smith (second from the left) joins the celebration in the winner's circle at Georgetown Raceway on July 24, 1971. (Courtesy of Hazell Smith.)

Georgetown Raceway is pictured in its former glory as it stands today, testing decades of erosion. The racetrack is in fair shape. In 2009, there was some speculation that the current owners wanted to resurrect the old raceway into a racino similar to Harrington and Dover Downs Raceways. (Author's collection.)

After Georgetown Raceway closed in 1972, Melvin Joseph used the facility for his own stable of Standardbred racehorses, building an indoor pool next to the stable area for therapeutic swimming and conditioning for his racehorses. Throughout the summer of 2012, Georgetown Raceway's grandstand was demolished. (Courtesy of the Author Lacey Lafferty.)

Four

Harrington Raceway

In 1919, a small group of civic-minded citizens met in the railroad station in Harrington and conceived the idea of having a fair in the area. These industrious men formed and planned the Kent and Sussex County Fair Association. During its first meeting on January 12, 1920, the association formed a corporation with capital stock, selling for $25 per share with the hope of being able to sell 1,200 shares. On February 17, 1920, the original land for the layout of the racetrack and grandstand, consisting of 30 acres, was purchased from William S. and Nellie Smith at a cost of $6,000. The first fair ran for four days and four nights, July 27 through July 30, with a carnival show in the grand midway. Harness racing was conducted on what was considered by racing officials to be one of the best half-mile tracks and grounds anywhere in the East. Plans proceeded almost immediately into the future, with a pledge to make next year's fair bigger and better than ever.

As years passed, horse race purses increased to encourage speed and good horses. In 1926, harness racing ran five days instead of four to accommodate the extra day of the fair. Through the years that followed, the fair board bought more acreage for the exhibits and needed repair and improvement to the main track. In 1946, as Kent and Sussex Raceway, it operated the first pari-mutuel harness racing meet in Delaware. In 1967, Kent and Sussex Raceway changed its name to Harrington Raceway. Today, it is the Harrington Raceway and Casino.

The track and racing surface have received a number of renovations over the years, perhaps most significantly in 2003. The speedy, half-mile oval was reconstructed prior to the 2003 spring meet by veteran track masters Dan and Greg Coon, who have been responsible for some of the most respected racetrack configurations in the nation. The restorations have resulted in broader turns and a securer, swifter racetrack.

The Delaware State Fair, a 10-day event usually in late July, started nearly a century ago. Traditionally, it holds a Governor's Day on the second Thursday of the Delaware State Fair, featuring a day of harness racing exclusively for Delaware-owned and-sired horses. Purses for the day have been as high as $700,000 and always draw a massive crowd in the grandstand as local horsemen compete for boastful rights on this special card of racing.

The first fair was held July 27–30, 1920, with a single admission of 50¢. This 1920s photograph of the Kent and Sussex Raceway and grandstand on the Harrington Fairgrounds shows hundreds of people seated and standing ready to watch the scheduled horse race events. The American farmer during the 1920s enjoyed a period of success that was created by World War I, when European nations required American agricultural exports to meet their demands due to a shortage of food. American family–owned farms grew in size along with agricultural production, which elevated higher prices for crops. Paired with new technologies and the mechanical modernization of farming equipment, agriculture became prosperous in United States. (Courtesy of Harrington Historical Society.)

A certificate of incorporation for the Kent and Sussex County Fair Association, Inc., was received in January. At a meeting on January 12, 1920, the association was organized and certificates of stock valued at $25 per share were issued with the hope of being able to sell 1,200 shares. The object of the corporation, as stated in the subscription to capital stock, was to have or manage a fair or exposition for the purpose of promoting and encouraging agriculture and giving pleasures and diversions to the inhabitants of rural communities within the state of Delaware. It now became the task of the 33 directors to buckle down and plan the first fair, a scant six months away. Diligent work began under the leadership of president Charles D. Murphy, vice president Ora C. Sapp, secretary Ernest Raughley, and treasurer William Smith. (Courtesy of Harrington Historical Society.)

A c. 1920s aerial photograph of the Kent and Sussex County Fair shows a horse race event taking place and several hundreds of people walking throughout the fairgrounds. Notice the number of vehicles parked on the fairground and surrounding properties. (Courtesy of Harrington Historical Society.)

Program of Classes and Purses

OF THE

Kent and Sussex County Fair Association, Inc.

HARRINGTON, DEL.

July 24, 25, 26, 27, 28, 1923

RACE		PURSE
	FIRST DAY, TUESDAY, JULY 24.	
No. 1.	2.22 Pace	$300.00
No. 2.	County Pace	300.00
No. 3	County Trot	300.00
	SECOND DAY, WEDNESDAY, JULY 25.	
No. 4.	2.13 Pace	300.00
No. 5.	2.14 Trot	300.00
No. 6.	2.20 Trot	300.00
	THIRD DAY, THURSDAY, JULY 25.	
No. 7	2.15 Pace	300.00
No. 8.	2.17 Trot	300.00
No. 9.	Free-For-All	300.00
No. 10.	2.18 Pace	300.00
	FOURTH DAY, FRIDAY, JULY 27.	
No. 11.	2.30 Pace	300.00
No. 12.	3 year old and under Trot	300.00
No. 13.	2.30 Trot	300.00

FIFTH DAY, SATURDAY, JULY 28.

AUTOMOBILE RACES ONLY.

Entries close July 16th, 1923. Entries made that day no bar

The fourth annual Kent and Sussex County Fair took place from July 24–28, 1923, with newspaper announcements of a premium list of classes, purses, and four days of horse racing. There was a high-class vaudeville show with the addition of fireworks every evening. (Courtesy of Matt Sparacino.)

This July 1937 photograph shows pacer Truman O. March at the Kent and Sussex County Fair preparing for the start of the race with trainer and driver George T. Satterfield in the bike. George Satterfield trained, raced, and bred a tough strain of harness horses known as the "March Standardbred" and was one of the first trainers and drivers at the Kent and Sussex County Fair. (Courtesy of Harrington Historical Society.)

Trotter Safe Palin is pictured before a race at the Kent and Sussex County Fairgrounds in the 1920s with G.C. Hootman in the bike. There were five days of horse racing and purse increases to encourage speed and good horses. (Courtesy of Harrington Historical Society.)

Pacer My Scott visits the winner's circle at Kent and Sussex Raceway with Paul Vinyard in the bike in the 1930s. Kent and Sussex Raceway manager Britt Holloway is standing in the background near the tower. There was a building on fair property called Vinyard Barn, most likely named after Paul. (Courtesy of Harrington Historical Society.)

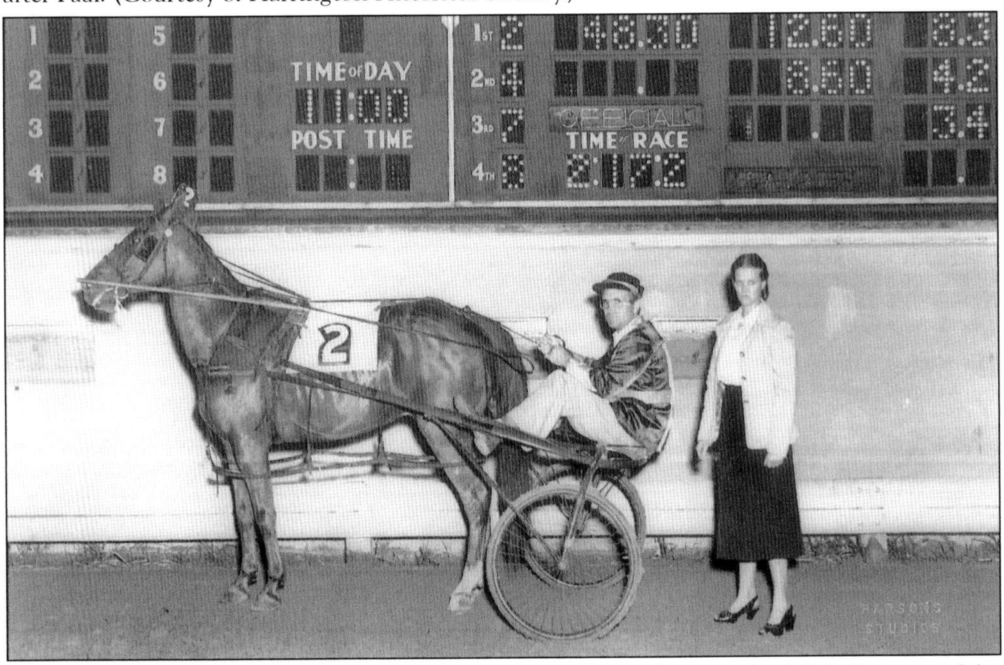

In the winner's circle at the Kent and Sussex Raceway is Percy Garey in the 1930s. Because of the Great Depression, purses were cut, premium awards were reduced, and box seat prices increased. (Courtesy of Harrington Historical Society.)

Harry "Boots" Morris holds a winner's trophy and blanket from his racehorse Gallant Heart's win at the Kent and Sussex Raceway in the 1930s. A big highlight in 1937 was a beauty contest to select Miss Delaware; Beatrice Harriett of Harrington won the title. (Courtesy of Harrington Historical Society.)

Pictured in the 1940s, these Kent and Sussex Raceway drivers are, from left to right, Tom Walters, Emil Adams, Tom Lewis, and Leslie Simpson. On Saturday, July 20, 1942, the *Journal-Every-Evening* headlined, "No Harrington Fair this Year," after a board of directors meeting when two military officers posed questions on patron safety due to the war in Europe. (Courtesy of Harrington Historical Society.)

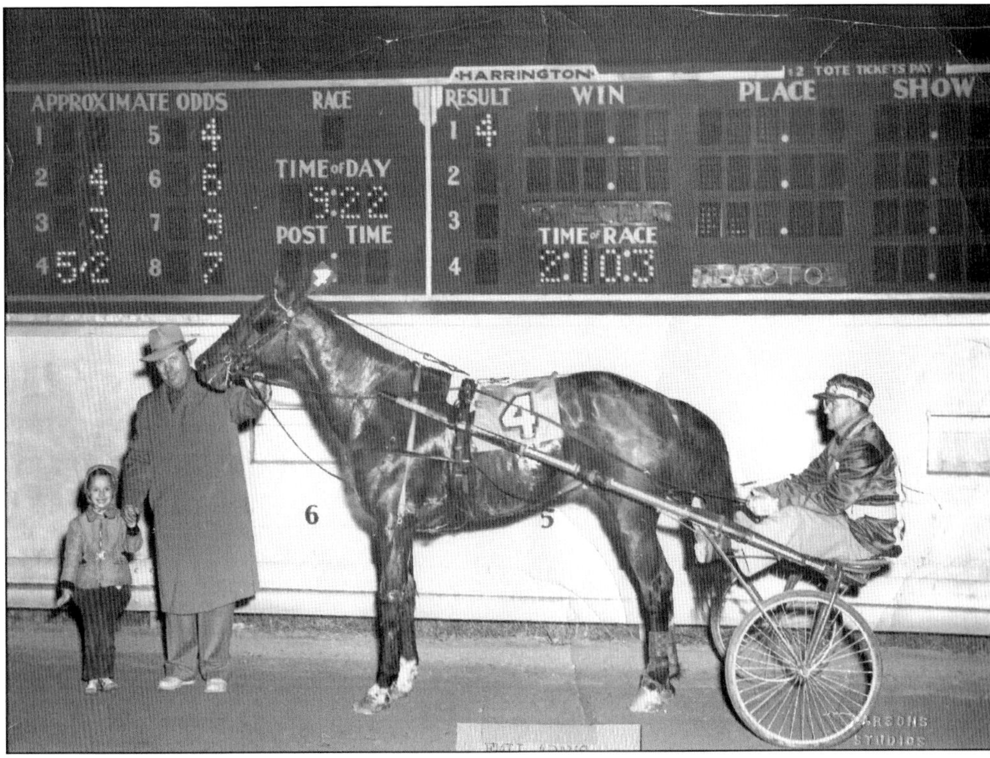

Driver Emil Adams drove his unknown trotter to a win. Pictured is his daughter Emmaline next to Earl Koons as they celebrate in the winner's circle at Kent and Sussex Raceway in the 1940s. In 1944, the fair board made an agreement with the US government to board 300 to 500 German prisoners of war for two months, while they worked at McNeil and Libby Cannery in Houston. (Courtesy of Harrington Historical Society.)

Driver Ernest M. Smith, Jean Miller's father, positions the gate car for the start of the race. In 1946, the Kent and Sussex Racing Association was organized to hold pari-mutuel racing in its fall meet. (Courtesy of Harrington Historical Society.)

Actor Robert Mitchum, who lived in and had grandparents in Felton, visits the winner's circle with an unidentified racehorse and driver in May 1948 at the Kent and Sussex Raceway. While establishing a career in Hollywood, Mitchum (far right) would make frequent trips to Felton, where he met his future wife, Dorothy Spence. They had three children. (Courtesy of Harrington Historical Society.)

Pacer Aristocracy wins in 2:12 with owner and driver J. Mallalieu in the bike for owner Quillen and Mallalieu on October 8, 1949, at the Kent and Sussex Fair. In February 1949, T. Brinton "Britt" Holloway was employed as general manager of the fair. (Courtesy of Matt Sparacino.)

This 1949 photograph shows an unidentified group and horse inside the winner's circle at the Kent and Sussex Raceway. In 1950, high school band concerts and a glorified musical production, *Fantasies of 1950*, dazzled grandstand audiences at the fair. (Courtesy of Harrington Historical Society.)

This photograph shows an unidentified horse and driver winning the 1949 Warren T. Moore Memorial at the Kent and Sussex Raceway. The man with a book in his hand in the stand is Pat Caulk, and on his right is Mr. Leatherman. (Courtesy of Harrington Historical Society.)

This 1949 Kent and Sussex County Fair photograph shows, from left to right, J. Gordan Smith, Gov. Bert Carvel, speaker Earl Sylvester, Alex Dupont Byard, and Sen. John Townsend. (Courtesy of Harrington Historical Society.)

The Kent and Sussex Raceway had occasional stock car races held at different times of the year. Melvin Joseph's No. 49 stock car wins with driver John "the Flying Dutchman" Stoltzfus on Labor Day 1950. (Courtesy of Joe Ann Adams.)

Owner Jonas H. Shoemaker visits the winner's circle with trotter Merry Scott, who finished in 2:12.2 with driver J. Mallalieu in the bike on October 3, 1951, at the Kent and Sussex Raceway. In 1954, the old grandstand would be torn down and a new all-steel grandstand would replace it for $259,625. (Courtesy of Matt Sparacino.)

Pictured in 1952 are Kent and Sussex Racing Association officials. From left to right are (first row) Essel Farlow, A.E. Leatherman, Harvey Griffith, Cecil Wheatley, Eldridge Lusey, J. Jester, George Enslen, John "Jack" Halloway, Jake Williams, Clarence Dyer, Gene Anderson, Earl Sylvester, Chemist Earlson, and Sid Gruelock; (second row) Doctor Cherry, Dale Fetrow, Clarence "Pat" Keyes, Dr. Harry McDaniel, William "Bill" Chambers, and T.B. "Britt" Holloway. (Courtesy of Harrington Historical Society.)

Owner, trainer, and driver George Brenneman is pictured on the bike with his son Carl "Flip" Brenneman holding trotter Titania Hanover in the winner's circle after finishing in 2:11 at the Kent and Sussex Raceway in 1953. Titania Hanover was also a competitive pacer and won several races at a trot and pace throughout the Delaware, Maryland, and Pennsylvania circuit. (Courtesy of Vicky Brenneman.)

In 1958, according to this bulletin, a Delaware racing license and winner photograph was free, whereas today, Delaware racing licenses are $50. In January 1959, approved plans were made to install a mezzanine floor to the grandstand for $59,990. The improvements would install mutual facilities and concession areas for racing fans. (Courtesy of Matt Sparacino.)

In 1956, driver Lindale Coverdale visits the winner's circle with his child on his lap. His family and friends are also there to share his win with an unidentified pacer at the Kent and Sussex Raceway. (Courtesy of Harrington Historical Society.)

Delaware governor Bert Carvel and his family sit in the grandstand of the Kent and Sussex County Fair in 1964. Governor Carvel was from the town of Laurel, where he had a thriving fertilizer business, and he served two terms as Delaware's governor from 1949 to 1953 and again from 1961 to 1965. (Courtesy of Harrington Historical Society.)

Pacer Tammy's Star wins in 2:10.4 with Elton White in the bike for owner Brenda J. (Lewis Bramble) McAllister's first win on October 20, 1966, at the Kent and Sussex Raceway. Richard "Dick" Lewis stands next to McAllister in the winner's circle. (Courtesy of Brenda Lewis Bramble.)

Trotter Lida Boot wins in 2:16 with Charles Ferranto in the bike for owner Theresa Nicotra on November 2, 1966, at the Kent and Sussex Raceway. Family and friends join the celebration in the winner's circle. Notice the abbreviation for Harrington on the winner's blanket. (Courtesy of Harrington Historical Society.)

On September 8, 1965, pacer Silk Lady visits the winner's circle, finishing in 2:06.3 with owner, trainer, and driver Olin Davis in the bike at the Kent and Sussex Raceway. In July 1966, the raceway would play double duty to a demolition derby during the fair, presented as a grandstand attraction. (Courtesy of Harrington Historical Society.)

In 1967, the Kent and Sussex Raceway changed its name to the Harrington Raceway. Trotter Swift Song jogs in the winner's circle after winning the race in 2:09.3 for owner Everett Brown with driver J.D. Dennis Sr. in the bike at Harrington Raceway on October 10, 1967. (Courtesy of Harrington Historical Society.)

Owner Wayne Wilkins's pacer Adios Verna visits the winner's circle at Harrington Raceway, finishing in 2:13.2 with trainer and driver David Brock in the bike on November 6, 1969. Adios Verna was an offspring of the legendary world champion Adios Harry from Greenwood, Delaware. (Courtesy Wayne Wilkins.)

A 1971 aerial photograph of Harrington Raceway and Fairgrounds shows how the facility has grown into a colossal complex. Notice US Route 13 at the upper left and the size of the back (south) track in comparison to the front (north) track. (Courtesy of Harrington Historical Society.)

Carl "Flip" Brenneman is holding pacer Mr. Lafayette after taking the win in 2:10.4 with driver George Brenneman in the bike. They raced for owners Victor Kowalski and Albert Pearson on September 30, 1971, at Harrington Raceway. (Courtesy of Vicky Brenneman.)

Pacer Napolad is all alone coming down the stretch to win in 2:10.3 with trainer and driver George Brenneman in the bike for owners Victor Kowalski and Albert Pearson on October 16, 1971, at Harrington Raceway. (Courtesy of Vicky Brenneman.)

Boots Wilkins (the first owner of Delmarva Raceway–Georgetown Raceway) sits on the bike with trainer and driver Richard Putz after winning on pacer Jute's Girl. They raced for owner Henry J. Vogt, finishing in 2:06.3 at Harrington Raceway on October 8, 1972. (Courtesy Eddie Lambden.)

Pacer Scout's Pride wins in 2:09.2 with trainer and driver Alfred Smith in the bike for owner Hazell Smith of Lewes on May 5, 1974, at Harrington Raceway. Notice the single-shaft, sulky bike. They were known to be treacherous and did not last long in the racing industry. (Courtesy of Hazell Smith.)

Trotter Janflora wins in 2:13.2 with owner, trainer, and driver Olin Davis in the bike on September 14, 1974, at Harrington Raceway. Family and friends joined in the celebration in the winner's circle with the presentation of a Delaware Owned and Delaware Foaled award plaque. (Courtesy Harrington Historical Society.)

Pacer Fortified charged down the home stretch to a winning photo finish in 2:05.4 with trainer and driver Norwood Truitt in the bike for owner Andres C. Gomez on October 6, 1974, at Harrington Raceway. Notice that all eight racehorses in the field are shown. (Courtesy of Harrington Historical Society.)

Howard Miller knew several sports and entertainment celebrities through engagements at Brandywine Raceway. While on a visit to Harrington Raceway on October 24, 1974, Howard met with hall-of-fame pitcher Rollie Fingers (of the Oakland A's) and had him sign his raceway program. (Courtesy of Michael Wirtschafter.)

Pacer Constant Combat rallies for the win in 2:03.1 with trainer and driver Frank Abbott in the bike for owner Carroll W. Johnson on October 26, 1975, at Harrington Raceway. Beginning in the 1970s, racetrack attendance began to diminish, as seen in this photograph. (Courtesy Harrington Historical Society.)

Trotter Chessie Duke pulls out the win in 2:15 with trainer and driver Roman Miller in the bike for owner James Freeney II as family and friends join the celebration in the winner's circle on October 2, 1976, at Harrington Raceway. (Courtesy of Roman Miller.)

Pacer Baywood T. Adios fights to the finish in 2:06.4 for owner William Sink (holding the horse) and Raymond Hitch with trainer and driver William Murray in the bike on April 30, 1977, at Harrington Raceway. World champion Adios Harry was the sire of Baywood T. Adios. (Courtesy of William "Gary" Sink.)

Five

Dover Downs Raceway

Everyone in Delaware knows Dover Downs Raceway and Speedway—now known as Dover International Speedway—which is located in the middle of the state in Dover. Since 1969, Dover Downs has been holding NASCAR races, and the track is known throughout the circuit as the "Monster Mile."

In the mid-1960s, three men had a vision: create a spectacular racing facility that not only showcased NASCAR races but also included horse racing. Industrialist John W. Rollins; construction contractor and stock car and harness horse enthusiast Melvin Joseph; and lawyer, politician, and horse enthusiast David P. Buckson formed a team that wanted to change racing in the First State. The group purchased a 204-acre farm owned by Thomas Murray, located on the east side of Route 13 (Dupont Highway). Their vision materialized into a dual-purpose facility with a five-eighth-of-a-mile dirt track for horse racing within a one-mile, high-banked, concrete-surfaced oval for auto racing. Joseph was the chief designer of the track and was assisted by Richard E. Haber, former chief engineer of the Delaware State Highway Department. At a cost of $12.5 million, construction was completed in 1969. For the first two years, from 1969 to 1971, Thoroughbreds raced at the massive complex. Through another property acquisition in the early 1970s, the US Trotting Association (USTA) pari-mutuel racing dates were acquired and moved to Dover Downs facility, where Standardbred racehorses have been the nightly wintertime entertainment to this day.

Through the decades, Dover Downs continues to host nightly harness racing while expanding its operations from a speedway and raceway to include a casino and hotel located next to the tracks. Live harness races are simulcast to tracks and other off-track betting locations across North America on each of the company's more than 140 live race dates. A typical harness racing season at Dover Downs begins in November and ends in April. Post times are usually 4:30 p.m. or 5:30 p.m.

The Progress Pace is Dover Downs's signature event. It began in 1996, and during its first seven races, most of the top sophomore pacers in the sport have participated. Aside from the Progress Pace, other stakes events regularly held at Dover Downs include the Matron Series, the Classic Series, and the Delaware Standardbred Breeders' Fund.

Work began in 1968 on Dover Downs from an engineering design by Melvin Joseph with assistance from Richard Haber, former chief engineer of the State of Delaware. However, the one-mile length of the track came from utilizing the maximum amount of farmland on the property. (Courtesy of Joe Ann Adams.)

With the assistance of a 35-ton crane, cables were used to fasten the construction equipment while on the 24-degree banking, aiding its traction and delivering a more profound surface. Shown in the photograph are the grandstand and clubhouse near completion in 1968. (Courtesy of Joe Ann Adams.)

Melvin Joseph construction crews are preparing the asphalt stock car surface on the one-mile, 24-degree banking speedway. As work progressed through 1968 into 1969, construction crews simultaneously installed a five-eighths dirt track for racehorses in the center of the speedway. (Courtesy of Joe Ann Adams.)

Upon completion of the graded track, Melvin Joseph construction crews added four layers of asphalt. In the mid-1990s, Joseph ripped up the asphalt surface due to a weakening top layer, creating potholes in the corners and installing a concrete replacement. The horse track is comprised of a fine, stone-dust surface for optimal performance. (Courtesy of Joe Ann Adams.)

Ralph Moody (right) looks on as Melvin Joseph points out and describes different features of Dover Downs's massive, unfinished facility. The project lasted two years, led by Melvin Joseph and his superintendent Leroy Betts. Completion was critical to meet the scheduled opening race date in July 1969. (Courtesy of Joe Ann Adams.)

Once the construction of Dover Downs was complete in 1969, the cost of the endeavor was $12.5 million. This photograph displays the grandeur of Dover Downs Raceway and Speedway, an incredible double-duty racetrack enterprise. (Courtesy of Joe Ann Adams.)

A 1970 aerial photograph of the Dover Downs Raceway and Speedway displays crowds of people in the back-stretch grandstands, where today there are grandstands circling the entire track that can seat more than 100,000 fans. The horse track is visible, and during a pari-mutuel meet, dirt is used to cover the speedway from the paddock area to the raceway so racehorses can cross over. (Courtesy of Joe Ann Adams.)

In the 1960s, there was still a big demand for horse racing, and the racetrack was well attended. As seen in this photograph, hundreds of people are in the wagering windows and seating area of the Dover Downs Raceway grandstand during a pari-mutuel meet in 1969. (Courtesy of Joe Ann Adams.)

Pictured in 1969 are the dining areas of the clubhouse in the colossal Dover Downs Raceway grandstand. In its first two years of operation, Thoroughbred racing was the initial desirability; later, attendance faded, and harness racing days were acquired. They continue to this day. (Courtesy of Joe Ann Adams.)

Fans could have a luxurious dinner in the clubhouse. A glass partition separates the areas of the grandstand and the clubhouse in this 1969 photograph during a racehorse meet. The tremendous view of the illuminated racetrack from the grandstand is amazing. (Courtesy of Joe Ann Adams.)

Pacer Peppy Wyn cruises to a muddy win in 2:10.4 with driver Carl "Flip" Brenneman in the bike for his father, owner and trainer George Brenneman, on December 30, 1972, at Dover Downs Raceway. When it begins to rain and the track gets sloppy, track officials advise drivers to place mud fenders on their bikes, as shown in the photograph at right. (Courtesy of Vicky Brenneman.)

Coming down the stretch in a tight duel to the finish is pacer Duly Dean for a win in 2:09 with trainer and driver David Brock in the bike for owner Hazell Smith on January 23, 1973, at Dover Downs Raceway. (Courtesy of Hazell Smith.)

Pacer Frosty Flash crosses the finish line first in 2:09.1 with trainer and driver Donald Robertson for owner Meldon Wilkins on January 12, 1973, at Dover Downs Raceway. Several family members and friends join the celebration in the winner's circle. (Courtesy of Georgetown Historical Society/ Nutter Marvel Museum.)

Pacer Peppy Wyn, a frequent winner, is in the winner's circle after finishing the race in 2:06.4 with driver Carl "Flip" Brenneman in the single-shaft bike for trainer and owner George Brenneman on March 24, 1974, at Dover Downs Raceway. Brenneman had won a prior race, and with his winning purse, he bought the single-shaft bike for $800. (Courtesy of Vicky Brenneman.)

Trainer and driver Roman Miller cruises to a win with Jovial George in 2:03.2 for owner Robert W. Leager Jr. on March 14, 1976, at Dover Downs Raceway. Family and friends join the winner's circle celebration. (Courtesy of Roman Miller.)

Pacer Mr. Forty Nine sails to an easy finish in the Bill and Ginny Park Pace Race in 2:03.3 with trainer and driver Art Wirsching for owner Melvin Joseph on November 24, 1978, at Dover Downs Raceway. From left to right are Kenny Adams, Gene Pusey, Joe Ann Adams, Robin Joseph, Landy Adams, Melvin Joseph Jr., and Melvin Joseph. The person holding the horse is unidentified. (Courtesy of Joe Ann Adams.)

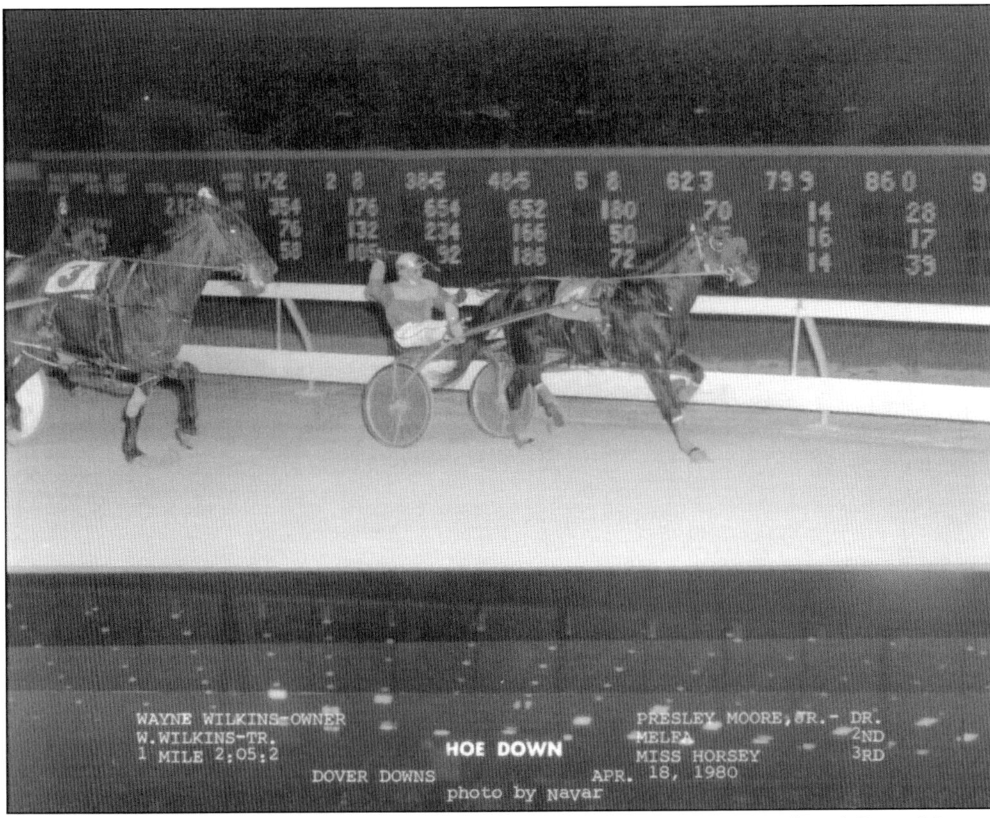

Owner Wayne Wilkins's Pacer Hoe Down is pictured racing down the stretch and holding on for the win in 2:05.2 with trainer and driver Presley Moore in the bike on April 18, 1980, at Dover Downs Raceway. Family and friends celebrated the well-deserved win. (Courtesy of Wayne Wilkins.)

Pacer Louis Easter fights off challengers for the win in 2:07.3 with driver Eddie Davis in the bike for owner Gardner King and trainer R. Putz on March 17, 1981, at Dover Downs Raceway. (Courtesy of Harrington Historical Society.)

Six

Delaware Park Raceway

Since its beginning in 1937, led by William Dupont Jr., Delaware Park Raceway has gone through many spectacular changes to reach its present-day operations; it has become a magnificent New Castle County centerpiece of excitement and place of intrigue in the world of horses.

The Delaware Racing Commission was created in 1933 and was given the control to grant licenses in 1935 for pari-mutal machines and receiving wagers in licensed horse races.

The Delaware Racing Commission gathered with the Delaware Steeplechase and Race Association, Inc., in 1936, creating a unified front to enhance the breeding of Thoroughbred horses and build a racetrack. A significant amount of land was purchased by the Delaware Steeplechase and Race Association, Inc., in Stanton, New Castle, Delaware, and was in the process of constructing a racing enterprise when a legislative bill was introduced and passed into law by the House and Senate, increasing the number of racing days from 20 to 30.

Delaware Park Raceway's earliest facilities were designed by William Dupont Jr., who had created 23 race courses, including a steeplechase course in Cecil County, Maryland, called Fair Hill Training Center. Delaware Park Raceway opened on June 26, 1937, with a 30-day meet showcasing the facilities with a 7,500-seat grandstand with a state-of-the-art clubhouse and Turf Club on the top level. The dirt track was a one-mile oval along with two steeplechase turf courses. The facility stabled 1,226 horses along the backstretch of the property, which enhanced the splendid overview of Delaware Park Raceway's impeccable structures, featuring the horses going to post and the picnic areas.

During World War II in 1943, Delaware Park Raceway was forced to close briefly even though the sport was blossoming and the community was embracing the harness racing business. After opening its doors in 1944, about 288,000 customers would emerge on Delaware Park Raceway spending more than $23 million, making the enterprise profitable.

A $2.8-million expansion was completed in 1958 that included a new clubhouse and expansion of the grandstand. Racing fans and horses were transported by B&O and Pennsylvania Railroads along the trackside terminals. Crowds of people converged upon Delaware Park Raceway from major metropolitan cities—20,000 individuals at the raceway was customary on the weekends.

Through decades of racing success and a temporary closer in 1982, William Rickman reopened the track in 1984.

In this photograph, Thoroughbred racehorses are seen charging down the stretch to the finish line at Delaware Park Raceway in front of thousands of eager fans on July 3, 1947. Inside the dirt track is a grass racetrack with jumps for the steeplechase events. A renowned Thoroughbred owner and horse breeder, Marion Dupont Scott, who managed Montpelier Stables, owned, raced, and boarded flat and steeplechase racehorses. A talented horsewoman, Scott grew up riding in Virginia and became interested in racing. She assisted her brother William Dupont in designing a number of racing sites including Delaware Park Raceway, Springdale Race Course in Camden, South Carolina, and Fair Hill Training Center in Maryland, which covers more than 5,000 acres and is where the National Steeplechase Association Headquarters is located. (Courtesy of Delaware Historical Society.)

In this photograph, hard-charging Realtor gains the lead on a sloppy dirt racetrack to win in the first race with Monogarny in second and Pango in third on June 14, 1947, at Delaware Park Raceway. Notice the thousands of racehorse fans that are packed in the grandstand and track-side areas. Delaware Park also hosts steeplechase events. Steeplechasing arrived in America via the sport of fox hunting and spread throughout the East Coast. (Courtesy of Delaware Historical Society.)

This view of the magnificent grounds of Delaware Park Raceway shows the massive size of the racetrack. Racehorses are running along the rail on May 30, 1949, after the eighth race. (Courtesy of Delaware Historical Society.)

An aerial view shows the massive complex of Delaware Park Raceway, including two steeplechase courses within the dirt racetracks, substantial barn areas, lots of vehicle parking spaces, and the railroad system behind the grandstand, where race fans and horses have easy excess to and from the facility. (Courtesy of Delaware Historical Society.)

Delaware Park Raceway has come a long way. From its inception in 1937 by William DuPont Jr., it has undergone many dramatic changes. Pictured sprinting to the finish line first is Croesus, followed by Our Sensation for second and Mason-Dixon for third on June 20, 1947. (Courtesy of Delaware Historical Society.)

Horse racing in North American dates to 1665, when a racetrack was constructed on Long Island, New York. These jockeys at Delaware Park Raceway gathered in celebration on June 24, 1958. They are, from left to right (by last name only), Russo, Lovato, Nelson, Choquette, and Cambers. (Courtesy of Delaware Historical Society.)

In this photograph, Thoroughbreds shift for position at Delaware Park Raceway on June 1, 1959. Delaware Park Raceway completed a $2.8-million expansion in 1958, including a new clubhouse, increasing the overall grandstands (and, in turn, increasing seating capacity), the addition of televisions, and the construction of the winner's circle. Famous Thoroughbred Barbaro—whose first race was at Delaware Park Raceway, which he won in October 2005—was trained by Michael R. Matz at Fair Hill Training Center. Ridden by Edgar Prado and Jose Caraballo, Barbaro went on to win five straight races, including the 2006 Kentucky Derby. For his achievements, Delaware Park Raceway began calling the Leonard Richards Stakes, a grade 3 race for three year olds, the Barbaro Stakes. Unfortunately, Barbaro was injured in the 2006 Preakness Stakes, breaking his right hind leg in three places and eventually succumbing to his injuries.

Bab's Way (left) is on the move and crossed the finish line victorious just seconds after the shutter snapped this three-horse fight to the finish. Cherwell took second for owners E. Dupont Weir and James C. Brady, resulting in third place going to Boom Boom. (Courtesy of Delaware Historical Society.)

Thousands of racehorse fans crowd into the main entrance of Delaware Park Raceway on June 4, 1952. Notice how close the railway train on the left side of the photograph is behind the raceway's entrance, making the facility easily accessible for people from all over the East Coast. (Courtesy of Delaware Historical Society.)

Dixiana Stables workers are pictured unloading Thoroughbred racehorses from Pennsylvania Railroad cars at Delaware Park Raceway in the 1950s. Trainloads of race fans came via the B&O and Pennsylvania Railroads to the trackside terminals. (Courtesy of Delaware Historical Society.)

The camera decided this race, the first four-way tie at Delaware Park Raceway. The decision went to Gwenywow (No. 1) on the rail with Dance-a-bit (No. 9) gaining second, Tunasman (No. 11) taking third, and Mill Tract (No. 2x) coming in fourth on June 18, 1954. (Courtesy of Delaware Historical Society.)

In the photograph, racehorse Trentonian looks over the *Telegraph* newspaper with caretaker Pinky Brown in the stables at Delaware Park Raceway on May 25, 1956. In 1993, William Rickman took control of the daily operations of the racetrack from his father. In the middle of the racing season, Delaware Park began transferring its simulcast signal to other tracks throughout the country, while offering local racing enthusiasts a schedule of numerous racing choices and a relaxed atmosphere for watching their favorite simulcast races. Over the past decade, Delaware Park has made several racing improvements to the facility including a recently resurfaced dirt racetrack and trimmed turf oval, a large infield video monitor, grandstand seat replacements, an outdoor grandstand ceiling enclosure, renovations to all the clubhouse levels, restorations to backside facilities, and, for betting ease, installation of Tiny Tim and BetJet betting games. (Courtesy of Delaware Historical Society.)

In this photograph, spirited two-year-old filly Billy Peg was a handful for exercise rider Bill Beatle on May 31, 1958, while leaving the stable area and entering the racetrack for her daily routine at Delaware Park Raceway. In the 1980s, Delaware Park enhanced family-oriented promotions, introduced local entertainment, and presented twin trifecta and Arabian racing. The Delaware General Assembly passed House Bill 628 in June 1994, The Horse Racing Redevelopment Act, which legalized slot machine gambling at Delaware racetracks. Under the control and guidance of the Delaware State Lottery Division, legislation was passed to introduce slots at Delaware Park Raceway, Dover Downs Raceway, and Harrington Raceway. With the future of horse racing looking bright, William Rickman developed plans to make Delaware Park one of the leading entertainment complexes in the state. (Courtesy of Delaware Historical Society.)

Here they come, charging down the stretch in the sixth race at Delaware Park Raceway on June 25, 1958. The person standing on a platform in the upper right of the photograph is presumed to be a racing official. (Courtesy of Delaware Historical Society.)

Delaware governor Walter Bacon is pictured with his business associates in the dining area of the Turf Club at Delaware Park Raceway on June 30, 1947. Governor Bacon served two terms from 1940 to 1948. (Courtesy of Delaware Historical Society.)

This photograph was taken from an adjacent building rooftop where Thoroughbred racehorses going to post before the Delaware Oaks event on June 11, 1959, at Delaware Park Raceway. Notice hundreds of fans lined along the hedges and hotel balconies circling the grounds. To increase the number of tracks receiving its simulcast signal during the live meet, in 1995, Delaware Park began a monumental promotional campaign to enhance its customer base. A year earlier, purses for live racing had been $48,000 per day, improved several times, and stretched to $92,000 per day at the end of the meet. The 1995 live racing season's total handle climbed to an all-time high of $91 million. William Rickman individually pursued efforts to gain video lottery legislation, which was passed while Delaware Park's simulcast operation flourished. (Courtesy of Delaware Historical Society.)

In the photograph, an unidentified Thoroughbred racehorse delivered an exceptional performance, pulling away from his competitors in the final stretch of the race on June 23, 1959 at Delaware Park Raceway. Notice the front-running horse's hooves are all off the ground. In 2009, the General Assembly, after much legal interpretation and numerous challenges, granted approval to Delaware Park Raceway to accept sports wagers. Within the same legislation was a clause to include table games in the future. This much-needed endeavor to produce new revenue and fresh faces added to the clubhouse's present-day environment. Delaware Park Raceway's first filled day of casino operations was on June 18, 2010, with 42 total games and a 20-table poker room. (Courtesy of Delaware Historical Society.)

Kelso (left) was a homebred foal for Allaire DuPont and raced for her Bohemia Stables his entire career. His lifetime record was 63 starts with 39 wins, 12 seconds, and two thirds. Trainer Carl Hanford (right) is escorting Kelso with Dick Jenkins at Delaware Park Raceway. It is arguable that there has been a horse before or since that has dominated racing for such a long period as Kelso. (Courtesy of Delaware Historical Society.)

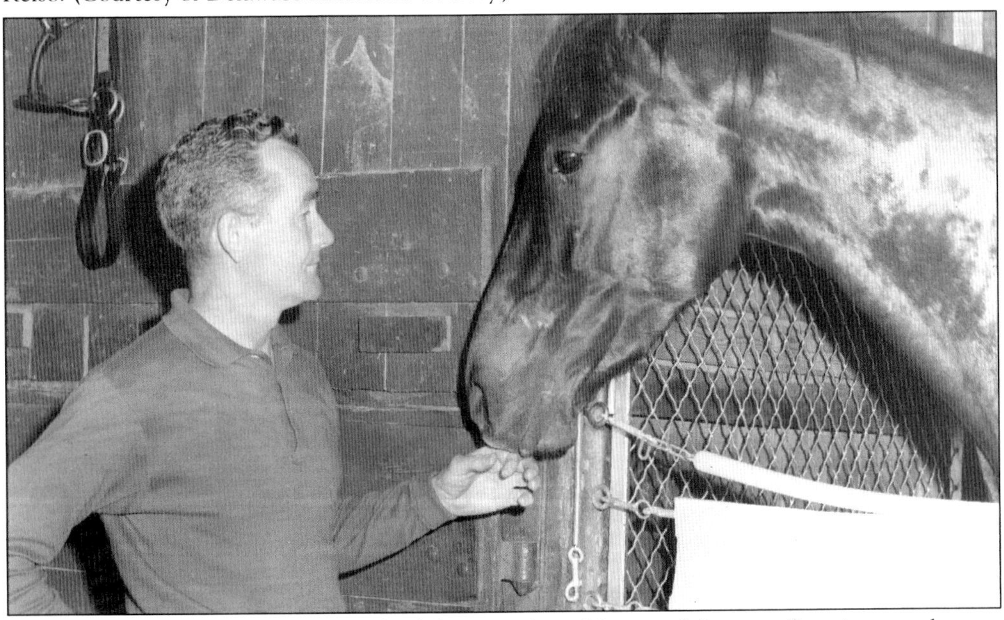

Kelso raced for eight years during which he was elected horse of the year five times and set or equaled 15 track records. In 1967, he was inducted into the National Museum of Racing and Hall of Fame—the most prestigious honor in American Horse Racing—and in 1977 he was inducted into the Aiken Thoroughbred Racing Hall of Fame. He was elected number four out of the top 100 US racehorses of the 20th century by the Aiken Thoroughbred Racing Hall of Fame. (Courtesy of Delaware Historical Society.)

Seven

Here They Come

At the beginning of a race, excitement fills the air and all eyes are focused on the starting line, waiting, waiting, until it is announced, "There they go" or "They're off." Fans follow intensely as the field approaches the first turn, watching their favorite racehorses. As the drivers or jockeys position their horses through the first and second turns, fans take a collective big breath and give a sigh of relief that all went well. As the field races down the backstretch, some fans begin talking to themselves, as if they were the drivers. Extreme levels of anxiety begins to overwhelm spectators, and instead of talking to themselves, they begin shouting out loud, "Come on, come on!"

At this point, most fans do not care how loud their voices are; everyone is feeling the same thing. Cheering their favorite racehorses to the front, fans watch as the animals race between the third and fourth turns. Drivers or jockeys begin to move and thrust their bodies with the rhythm of their mounts, hearing some talk to their horses, others shouting, "Yah, yah!"

The horses begin to fan out across the track. Coming out of the fourth turn, the announcer cries, "Here they come!" Drivers or jockeys try to find a hole to get their mounts through, weaving their way through traffic and barreling down the front stretch. All hearts are beating as fast as a brass band as fans' favorite horses make their moves towards the finish line. At that moment, it is the adrenaline rush that brings fans to the races and keeps them coming back for more.

Everyone wants their favorite horse to win the race. But whether the horse came in first, second, or last, that mighty beast gave all it had so fans could have a moment of thrilling excitement, and for that, the horse is to be commended. After all, the racehorse is the show, everything else is the stage.

Cindy's Royce wins the President's Race in 2:03 with driver Joe Dugan Jr. in the bike for owners Richard Sr. and Gary Brandley on November 12, 1988, at Harrington Raceway. Sen. Thurman Adams is fourth from the right and Gary Simpson is second from the right. (Courtesy of Matt Sparacino.)

Happy To Be In Town wins the Governor's Cup in 2:00.2 at the Delaware State Fair–Harrington Raceway with driver Herve Filion for owners Jay, Robert and Jeffrey Breasure on July 26, 1990. (Courtesy of Matt Sparacino.)

Trainer Jeffrey Cox's Cambest Prince wins the Governor's Cup in 1:54 at the Delaware State Fair–Harrington Raceway with driver Greg Grismore for owners Samual R. Jacobs and Charles Burris Jr. on July 24, 2003. Delaware governor Ruth Ann Minner presents the trophy and behind her is Sen. Thurman Adams. (Courtesy of Matt Sparacino.)

Strong Scooter wins the President's Cup in 1:53.4 with trainer and driver Toby Lynch Jr. in the bike for owner Alton E. Lynch Jr., Inc., on July 24, 2003, at the Delaware State Fair–Harrington Raceway. Matt Sparacino, the assistant general manager of Harrington Raceway, is first on the left, Patricia Key, the chief executive officer of Harrington Raceway, is fifth from the right, and William Chasanov, the president of Harrington Raceway, is second on the right. (Courtesy of Matt Sparacino.)

Trainer Linda McDonald's Willie T wins the "In Memory of Walter Messick" in 2:04.1 with driver Eddie Davis Jr. in the bike for owner Medford Davis Jr. on July 23, 2003, at the Delaware State Fair–Harrington Raceway. Race fans, friends, family, and raceway directors join the winner's circle celebration. (Courtesy of Matt Sparacino.)

Trainer Robert Nibblett Jr.'s pacer Western Genius wins the 11th race in 1:55 with driver Ross Wolfenden in the bike for owners Robert Nibblett and William "Gary" Sink at Dover Downs Raceway on February 28, 2004. (Courtesy of William "Gary" Sink.)

Western Game wins the ninth race in 1:55.1 with Cory Callahan in the bike for owner and trainer Lou Johnson on February 14, 2010, at Dover Downs Raceway. Lou Johnson (first on the right) is from Georgetown and is a five-time late model track champion at the Delaware International Speedway and currently drives his late model stock car at Delaware International Speedway in Delmar. (Courtesy of Lou Johnson.)

Owner and trainer Lou Johnson's KP's Kruzer wins the 12th race in 1:58.3 with Ross Wolfenden in the bike on April 25, 2010, at Harrington Raceway. From the right are unidentified, Shawn Elliott, Bobby Smith, driver Ross Wolfenden, Lou Johnson, and Judy Johnson. (Courtesy of Lou Johnson.)

Georgetown businessman and horseman Melvin Joseph gives his Standardbred racehorse Tyler's Point a treat in 1995. Tyler's Point had a successful racing career in Florida and was retired to Melvin's Georgetown farm, located next to his construction business. (Courtesy of Joe Ann Adams.)

Drivers Corey Callahan (front) and Victor Kirby (back) duel it out down the stretch towards the finish line at Harrington Raceway in the late 2000s. Callahan has been the leading driver several times at Delaware tracks and participated in the World Driving Championship in 2011, placing second. Kirby received the Delaware Standardbred Owners Association (DSOA) 2000 Horizon Star award and operates a successful racing stable in Delaware. (Courtesy of Megan Warnick.)

Pacer Wayne Rainy captured the win in the 12th race in 1:57.3 with driver George Dennis in the bike for owner Wayne G. Wilkins and trainer Delbert Richards Jr. on September 28, 2006, at Harrington Raceway. (Courtesy of Wayne Wilkins.)

Seattle Sleu wins an event at Delaware Park Raceway on March 6, 1980—not to be confused with the 1977 Triple Crown winner Seattle Slew. Unidentified owners, fans, family, and friends are pictured in the winner's circle. (Courtesy of Delaware Historical Society.)

Owner and trainer Scott Peck's Hobo Adios captured the win in 2:02 with driver Brian Manges in the bike on May 18, 1983, at Brandywine Raceway. Joining the celebration are Perry Friend, Scott Peck, Grace Lafferty (white shirt), Pete Marsh, and Betty Peck (dark jacket). Peck trained Standardbreds and Thoroughbreds for over 30 years throughout the East Coast and was president of Delaware Thoroughbred Horse Association (DTHA) for six years. (Courtesy of Scott Peck.)

Owner and trainer Scott Peck's Smokie captures the win in 1:46.1 with Scott's daughter jockey Donna Peck on August 12, 2002, at Delaware Park Raceway. Joining the celebration are Katie Couchman, Burt Piecuch, Doug Hawkins, D. Scott Peck, Russell Reynolds (under the horse's neck), and Scott Peck. (Courtesy of Scott Peck.)

Trainer Brenda Lewis Bramble's pacer Southview Whitney is pictured charging to the finish in 1:55.2 with Corey Callahan in the bike for owner Lloyd H. Hickman at Harrington Raceway on August 24, 2010. Hickman privately purchased Southview Whitney from Prince Edward Island, Nova Scotia. Hickman has been involved in the horse racing industry for more than 50 years throughout Delaware and the surrounding areas. In the 1950s, he trained and campaigned racehorses for Tom Lewis for several years; however, he later became employed by the state of Delaware and took a hiatus from racing. After retiring from the state, Lloyd decided to get involved again with horse racing, privately purchasing and claiming several racehorses in the last 12 years for trainer Brenda Lewis Bramble. One of his earlier claimers and favorite racehorses is retired Doctor A.B., whom he describes to have a unique domineering personality when he is in the company of other horses in his pasture. Lloyd currently owns and operates Hickman Package Store in Ocean View. (Courtesy of Brenda Lewis Bramble.)

Trainer William "Billy" C. Haggerty's pacer Winbak Transfer holds on for the win in 1:56.3 with Tony Morgan in the bike for owner Lacey Lafferty (holding daughter Lacey Lynn) on June 12, 2007 at Harrington Raceway. Billy's father, on the far right, is owner and trainer William Haggerty. The Bobby Quillen Memorial is a Harrington Raceway signature event that occurs every year, showcasing harness racing's top aged performers from different parts of the country. The race is titled after an admired Delaware legislator and tenured Harrington Raceway board member, who was a devout supporter of horseman rights and a regular at the half-mile raceway. Harrington Casino underwent a $40-million major expansion project in 2007 that created a modern-day appearance while increasing the size of the gaming area and aiding the start of table games, which were added in 2010. (Author's collection.)

The Delaware Standardbred Breeders' Fund Stakes one-day-old colt Sombodydonsombody, also known as Trooper, stands safely next to his mother, Jaguar's Lady, on May 26, 2011. The Delaware Standardbred Breeders' Fund administrator vigorously pursues the competitive level of race purses and supervises the sires program and racing program that includes sixteen $100,000 races per year equally divided between Dover Downs Raceway and Harrington Raceway. The Delaware Standardbred Breeders' Fund also promotes Delaware-bred horses in distinguished Standardbred sales throughout the East and encourages support of educational affairs like the Harness Horse Youth Camp and the annual New Owners Seminar, along with numerous events around the state. Governor's Day is the Delaware Standardbred Breeders' Fund's signature event at the state fair, held on a Thursday in July. The 2012 Governor's Day harness racing event exceeded expectations and marked the first-time occasion a success. (Author's collection.)